POETRY RE[V]

AUTUMN 1996 VOLUME

EDITOR PETER FORBES
PRODUCTION MARTIN DR
SUBSCRIPTIONS AND ADVERTISING SOPHIE JEFSON

GW00357744

CONTENTS

LONDON MAGAZINE

FICTION * MEMOIRS * CRITICISM * POETRY
CINEMA * ARCHITECTURE * PHOTOGRAPHY
THEATRE * ART * MUSIC

'A fantastic magazine whose place in the history of 20th century literary life grows ever more secure and significant' – *William Boyd, Evening Standard*

Each issue contains over 50 pages of poems and reviews of poetry.

Recent and forthcoming critical essays include:

C. K. Stead on Craig Raine and Thom Gunn

Alan Ross on Derek Walcott and St. Lucia

Marshall Walker on Edwin Morgan

Michael O'Neill on Stephen Spender and Gavin Ewart

Dennis O'Driscoll on Berryman and Yeats

Subscriptions:
£28.50 p.a. (six issues) to 30 Thurloe Place, London SW7

Single copies £5.99 from discriminating bookshops

POETRY REVIEW SUBSCRIPTIONS
Four issues including postage:

UK individuals £23
Overseas individuals £31
(all overseas delivery is by airmail)
USA individuals $56

Libraries, schools and institutions:
UK £30
Overseas £37
USA $66

Single issue £5.95 + 50p p&p (UK)

Sterling and US dollar payments only. Eurocheques, Visa and Mastercard payments are acceptable.

Bookshop distribution:
Password Books
Telephone 0161 953 4009

Design by Philip Lewis

Typeset by Poetry Review

Printed by Warwick Printing Co Ltd at Theatre Street, Warwick CV34 4DR and at 112 Bermondsey Street, London SE1 3TX
Telephone 0171 378 1579

POETRY REVIEW is the magazine of the Poetry Society. It is published quarterly and issued free to members of the Poetry Society. Poetry Review considers submissions from non-members and members alike. To ensure reply submissions must be accompanied by an SAE or adequate International Reply coupons: Poetry Review accepts no responsibility for contributions that are not reply paid.

Founded 24 February 1909
Charity Commissioners No: 303334
© 1996

THE POETRY SOCIETY

EDITORIAL AND BUSINESS ADDRESS:
22 BETTERTON STREET, LONDON WC2H 9BU

telephone **0171 240 4810**
fax **0171 240 4818**
email **poetrysoc@dial.pipex.com**

ISBN 1 900771 02 0
ISSN 0032 2156

Funded by THE ARTS COUNCIL OF ENGLAND

STRANGE ATTRACTION

IAN SANSOM WELCOMES A NEW ANTHOLOGY OF AVANT GARDE POETRY
(BUT NOT THE INTRODUCTION)

Conductors of Chaos
ed. Iain Sinclair,
Picador, £9.99,
ISBN 0 330 33135 3

DON'T BE PUT OFF by Iain Sinclair's silly and self-important introduction to this otherwise marvellous anthology of contemporary poetry. Some of what Sinclair has to say is good knock-about stuff – he dismisses the Movement, for example, as an "alimentary spasm", describes the New Generation Poets as "pod people", has the obligatory dig at Motion and Morrison's *Penguin Book of Contemporary Poetry*, and even lays into Michael Horovitz's *Children of Albion*, denouncing them as a bunch of fakers: "the Carshalton chapter of the Dharma Bums, flotsam from Nottingham Dale, and a few blokes Horovitz met in the pub". But the glorious bombast turns to drivel when Sinclair starts running on about "poet-shamans" producing "joyous exorcisms of polluted public spaces" and other

such mystifying clap-trap, which is presumably meant to make poetry sound radical and exciting but actually just makes Sinclair sound like a tired old hippy. "The work I value", he explains, "is that which seems most remote, alienated, fractured . . . The darker it grows outside the window, the worse the noise from the island, the more closely do I attend to the mass of instant-printed pamphlets that pile up around my desk". He should get out more.

But then again someone needs to sit at home sifting through the little magazines and the small-press publications and Sinclair does a better job than most. He even claims to enjoy it. "The very titles", he enthuses, "are pure adrenalin: *Satyrs and Mephitic Angels, Tense Fodder, Hellhound Memos, Civic Crime, Alien Skies, Harpmesh Intermezzi, A Pocket History of the Soul*". *Tense Fodder* pure adrenalin? For all his burbling, Sinclair manages to rescue the work of a number of poets below the care of reputation and beyond the pale of mainstream publishing, whose productions would otherwise have been given up to the greedy jaws of the book-lice. There is, admittedly, some overlap between the poets featured in his anthology and the poets in the two infamous Paladin anthologies of the late 1980s and early 1990s, Andrew Crozier and Tim Longville's *A Various Art* and Gillian Allnutt et al's *the new british poetry*, which served to remind readers of the range of British poetry written in a neo- and post-modernist fashion. Thus, readers have already had a chance to make up their minds about the likes of Brian Catling, Cris Cheek, Kelvin Corcoran, Andrew Crozier, Andrew Duncan, Allen Fisher, Bill Griffiths, Lee Harwood, John James, Barry MacSweeney, Geraldine Monk, Douglas Oliver, J. H. Prynne, Maggie O'Sullivan, Denise Riley, Peter Riley, and John Wilkinson. But Sinclair also offers up new(-er) voices, including Stewart Home, Grace Lake and Drew Milne, as well as a selection of work from "significant poets from previous generations" (David Gascoyne, Nicholas Moore, J. F. Hendry, W. S. Graham and David Jones). It is very much a tribal gathering.

Deciding about the merits of this sort of coming together is a tricky business. In certain circles to admit to a taste for the poetry of, say, Jeremy Prynne or Barry MacSweeney is like admitting to a taste for raw sewage, while champions of "alternative" poetries tend to go apoplectic at the mere mention of the names of Raine or Heaney or Harrison. In an article rebarbartively titled 'What Is Wrong Now With English Poetry' Michael Horovitz once claimed that "Any of Craig Raine's inexorably formulaic toss-offs he can't get sucked up by any other paper will be guaranteed overnight insemination by the *Observer*, courtesy of old pal Blake (BLAKE!) Morrison". This isn't polemic, it's pub-talk, having nothing whatsoever to do with poetry, and everything to do with belonging to a club, and with demonising and denigrating the "enemy". In 1987 the magazine *Reality Studios* invited readers to "submit a list of up to three of their favourite/most significant books of poetry published in the 1980s". There were just 24 entries, most of them from poets – including Peter Finch, Michael Horovitz, Lee Harwood, John Wilkinson, Maggie O'Sullivan and Kelvin Corcoran – nominating each other's work (Peter Riley boldly rejected such nepotism and plumped instead for straight solipsism: he nominated a book he'd written himself). The poetry world is a small world: small, nasty and brutish.

And yet beyond all the back-slapping and the in-fighting there are lots of good things happening. Certainly, some of the material in *Conductors of Chaos* is second-rate – work produced by egg-heads minus the yolk – and there's perhaps a little too much zany stuff, too much typographical ejaculation, too much that is half-digested, too much poetry like chyme (the creamy acid fluid made up of partly digested foods and gastric juice that forms in the stomach). But there is also much that is intelligent, well-formed and refreshing, including beautiful lyrics from the likes of Rod Mengham and Denise Riley, some extraordinary long poems and poem series, including Cris Cheek's 'Stranger' and Lee Harwood's 'Cable Street', and some serious political and social-realist verse by Kelvin Corcoran ("Estate by estate, family by family / the poor turned invisible, / in the hard blue sky above the stadium / currencies vanish, nations appear") and Andrew Duncan ("They're upping the output norms, / Sending the lines offshore, tearing off the payrolls / And asking for maths. / The factories are closing and there aren't / Even yards you could sweep out / or pallets you could stack").

The main difference between the kind of poetry represented in *Conductors of Chaos* and that in a comparable anthology such as Bloodaxe's *The New Poetry*, is not so much a difference in subject-matter or even in method, but simply in manner, or in tone, in what one might call the "attitude" of the verse. Where *The New Poetry* proudly offered "accessibility, democracy and responsiveness" Sinclair's selection is much more inhospitable and unwelcoming, and deliberately so. Sinclair's poets aren't writing to please, aren't writing to be read in schools or applauded in clubs or on TV; if anything, they're writing to slow you down and trip you up, and even to offend. Brian Catling's magnificent long poem 'The Stumbling Block its Index' is precisely about the pros and cons of poetry as *skandalon*:

> **The Stumbling Block** has been used like an entrance step to sharpen knives on. Its fossil bristle of tight stone forcing the heavy blades down to a hiss along one edge. These are knives of gleaming hubris, long intentions honed for malice. They are magnetised and have been placed to construct a lectern. Each blade holding the next to form the platform. It may hold this index at its centre, hovering, placed outside in the aorta of streets. The removal of any of the blades from the assembled cluster will spill their fish bodies to the ground. The paper will drink any of the stains of their usage.

Of course, "difficulty" always was, and remains, a key feature in modernist poetry and in poetry inspired by modernism (Eliot: "Poets in our civilisation, as it exists at present, must be difficult"), and on the whole it's a good thing: poems should make you work a bit, should make you think, should resist sheer transparency and simple paraphrase. Inevitably, there are poets in *Conductors of Chaos* who get carried away and refuse to say anything intelligible at all – they fail to conduct their own chaos – or who are content to make the same dull points again and again and again: there is no simple sense of voice, no simple self, no simple correspondence between life as we live it and the work of art. They produce "difficult" poems, poems which refuse to make clear statements and refuse to answer questions, and end up sounding like poorly briefed politicians. But there are others in the anthology – one thinks of Stephen Rodefer and Michael Haslam – who write complex work, yet who still manage to communicate and to achieve a great deal of clarity, a clarity not perhaps on the level of ideas, but in the arrangement of words on the page (it is no surprise that many of Sinclair's poets are painters or performance artists). Such work is not susceptible to paraphrase, or even to quotation. It is, in a sense, unteachable. Which means you have to read it instead.

Poetical Correctness

EDNA LONGLEY ANATOMISES TWO BOOKS WHICH ATTEMPT TO
THEORISE THE POETRY OF THE LAST FIFTEEN YEARS

DAVID KENNEDY
New Relations: The Refashioning of British Poetry 1980–1994

Seren Books,
hbk £19.95, ISBN 1 85411 162 0
pbk £9.95, ISBN 1 85411 163 9

IAN GREGSON
Contemporary Poetry and Postmodernism: Dialogue and Estrangement

Macmillan,
hbk £30, ISBN 0 333 65565 6
pbk £14.99, ISBN 0 333 65566 4

THESE STUDIES BROACH the problem of criticism and contemporary poetry – especially poetry from England. Ian Gregson and David Kennedy are worried about the divergent languages spoken by what we might call "the poetry world" and by the academy. Thus they try to come up to speed on the theoretical front while also showcasing the work of new, newish or neglected poets. Since post-structuralism sits uneasily with puffery, this agenda involves contradictions. But if the outcome appears more symptomatic than therapeutic, it is mainly because of biases that marginalise critical discrimination and a sense of literary history. As so often, hard (or supposedly hard) theory colludes with soft criticism: a collusion epitomised by Kennedy's earnestly correct use of "poetries" and "Englishes" (do music critics refer to "musics"?). Although I sympathise with his objection to "cults of the personal and the real", and with his regret that "the public intellectual" ignores poetry, his book rehearses a familiar kind of English over-reaction against English Wordsworthianism. That is, he vaults from subjectivity to sociology at the expense of aesthetic and cultural intricacies that both emphases miss. Gregson's argument takes another well-worn path: the discovery of early twentieth century modernism as if it had occurred yesterday. Each critic bestows on certain effects in contemporary poetry a radical status they have hardly earned. English criticism follows English politics into

binary oppositions. Gregson stakes all on an antithesis between "realism" and postmodernism or "self-reflexive fictiveness". Self-reflexiveness has been around in lyric poetry since Horace and takes as many different forms as poems have "selves". Further, like Kennedy, Gregson makes Philip Larkin the benchmark of realism, without considering either the complexity of Larkin's voices and symbols or whether realism is a term applicable to poetry. (It is true, if irrelevant, that bad writing is now more likely to posture as postmodernist than as close to the social coalface.) Kennedy is equally muddled when he speaks of "the dominant realist surface being broken down" in 1980s collections by Peter Didsbury, Sean O'Brien and Michael Hofmann. Citing such qualities as "ironic levity" – presumably a thing never known before – or the dissolution of the self into a "linguistic and historical 'internet'", he quotes O'Brien's remark that they constitute "the earned surplus" of the realism of "the middle generation". This inappropriately progressive model (the middle generation here signifies Dunn, Harrison, and Heaney) casts much of twentieth century poetics into limbo. I confess that I cannot see O'Brien's rather longwinded verse as any kind of advance on Larkin. Kennedy then praises O'Brien's "It all depends what you mean" as an example of "resistance to traditional closure". To adapt Larkin, nothing, like something, happens in any poetic manner.

Gregson's subtitle defers to the over-fashionable theories of Bakhtin and Shklovsky. Bakhtin's dialogism was, in fact, expressly designed to elevate the novel over poetry, and a search for poetic models of dialogue, dialectic, intertextuality, masks, carnivalesque and drama need look no further than the theory and practice of W. B. Yeats. As for estrangement or defamiliarisation, it should not entail the strained surrealism often commended by Gregson. And while he devotes some chapters to poets worth talking about (Edwin Morgan, James Fenton, Fleur Adcock), he forces their work into unnecessary contortions: "What makes 'Chosun' so radical is that it makes heteroglossia coincide with what Foucault calls heteropia". At one point, his scheme obliges him to encourage the pretensions of Veronica Forrest-Thompson; at another, to write about Fleur Adcock's poetry as "unsettling any reliable sense of ontological stability". Gregson admits that what he terms "the mainstream" has been infiltrated by modernist premises. In which case he should have abandoned his scheme, together with his innocence about the politics of canons inside and outside the university.

Kennedy coins a stylistic binary that would have astonished Cicero: i.e. between "auditory" and "rhetorical" modes – the latter allegedly practised by Simon Armitage and Glyn Maxwell. Here again belief in progress imposes premature significance on uneven if lively *oeuvres*. He seems to mean that these poets hear no inner voice (unprovable), but "share an interest in the use of cliché for both comic and ironic effect...Their poetries also borrow from both non-literary (media, advertising) and non-cultural (commerce, sport) discourses". Edmund White has written that "Of all languages English is the wittiest, since it not only permits but craves sudden shifts in tone, the downshifting from the hieratic to the demotic" (*London Review of Books*, 22 August). In recent times Auden and MacNeice come to mind as highlighting such shifts and "discourses". Perhaps Kennedy's failure to remember the Thirties stems from the fact that *New Relations* was written to complement *The New Poetry* (1993) of which he was an editor. History begins in the 1980s and earlier decades, older poets, recede into antique mists.

As in the introduction to *The New Poetry*, Kennedy equates cultural pluralism with "pluralism of poetic voice" and indexes British (English) poetry to the condition of Britain (England) – though without drawing on thinkers like Patrick Wright or Neal Ascherson. Thus he generally sees poetry as paralleling trends towards post-colonialism, classlessness and deconstruction of the metropolitan centre. His gurus are not the Russian formalists but Fanon and Said. Kennedy writes, for example: "We might say that rather than *wishing* [like Tony Harrison] to be the poet his father reads, Armitage simply gets on with the job of *being* that poet". We might say, alternatively, that Harrison has flogged a certain subject matter to death, and that discussion of both his and Armitage's poetry should develop in other terms. In his own terms, as well as mine, Kennedy is surely on dodgy ground when he announces: "I have chosen not to write about Black British or Afro-Caribbean poetry not only because it seems inappropriate for a white critic to do so but because these poetries are still being theorised through perspectives of language and difference". In thus fragmenting the art and avoiding value-judgements Kennedy sounds patronising rather than open to all the possibilities of poetry.

Both books are, indeed, confused about the relation of poetry to English multiculturalism, the British Isles and Abroad. Whereas in Irish criticism foreign countries and foreign poets can be a code for declaring independence of Eng. Lit., in English criticism post-Imperial guilt mingles with a belief that America is less provincial than the UK and that continental Europe holds the intellectual cure for English/British insularity. There is some truth in both these (longstanding) beliefs, but they may evade rather than promote indigenous self-awareness. If there is an English crisis, and if poetry's horizons are relevant to it, we require more than the information that "John Ash . . . was born in Manchester but relocated to New York at the start of the 1980s; Frank Kuppner is a Scot of Polish extraction; and Michael Hofmann is an Anglo-German". Later, Kennedy does begin to ask deeper questions about Blake Morrison's fawning construction of an "international superleague" and about the problematic prestige or, as he puts it, "symbolic capital" associated with foreign contexts, contacts and allusions.

Assumptions about *caelum* and *animus* are revealing when it comes to Irish poetry. This is an internationalism that does not know its next-door neighbour (to be fair, Ireland often returns the compliment). Gregson tells us that "although Muldoon shares Heaney's rural background, he does not share his awed yet anxious respect for nature, and has grown increasingly cosmopolitan and urbane (he now lives in America and teaches at Princeton University)". This gives the impression that Heaney and Muldoon attended a hedge school before being airlifted into the Ivy League. Muldoon may have acquired some rudimentary "urbanity" through living in Belfast, going to university there, and working for BBC Northern Ireland. Significantly, although Kennedy and Gregson mostly avoid Ireland – Kennedy says that Irish poetry has been "more than adequately covered and theorised" – each poaches an Irish poet to boost his case. Gregson's chapter on Muldoon has little new to say and misreads his textual politics: "Despite his apolitical stance . . . Muldoon sympathises with Heaney's nostalgia for a lost Irishness". Kennedy represents Heaney, Harrison and Dunn as culturally indistinguishable, and post-structuralism takes a breather while he applauds "the identification of voice with the soil of a particular place", or uses Heaney's writings as his sole authority on Irish culture and Anglo-Irish literary relations. Kennedy modestly proposes that he has made an "original contribution" on Heaney. In fact, he proceeds as virtually every English critic has done since the publication of *Death of a Naturalist.*

Coming to terms with poetic interactions between England and Ireland (or England and Scotland) demands more than appropriating one Celtic poet per generation. And history, together with the shorter distances between the roles of poet, academic and intellectual in a small country, has propelled Irish debates faster down the critical path which these books seek to signpost.

JAAN KAPLINSKI

"Saying everything, almost equal to being able to say nothing, and saying anything, a basically uncommunicative conception of language, has made J. Kaplinski's most recent poetry a fount of ineptitude and unintelligibilty, and of the author himself a singer in the wilderness for whom the gap between recognition and understanding is reaching its frontier" – Linnar Priimägi

On the border between recognition and understanding
sometimes this side, sometimes that, sways J. K.
in the autumn wind, like the dry stem of a meadowsweet.
When he writes, on the far side of the border of intelligibility.
When he makes porridge, washes the clothes or washes his face,
presumably on the near side. Close to the border
measurements, distances and qualities alter.
Things get mixed up, soap doesn't lather,
water boils at room temperature, ice doesn't melt,
ermine stays white in summer and art seems so artistic
that J. K. wants to write himself free of art,
write himself free of himself. Everything around him
becomes ever more distant – newspapers, children, books,
everything becomes less his own; the distant
is even clearer and sharper, while what is close by
becomes hazy, books difficult to read, and what is closest of all
dissolves completely, so
you point your finger and probe the part of the room
where your body or soul should be,
but there's no trace of either.
Presumably poetry has reached its goal.

Damned to Fame

WE PRINT HERE A PREVIOUSLY UNPUBLISHED SAMUEL BECKETT POEM AND AN EXTRACT
FROM JAMES KNOWLSON, *DAMNED TO FAME: THE LIFE OF SAMUEL BECKETT.* THIS
EXTRACT RELATES TO THE TIME AT WHICH THE POEM WAS WRITTEN. BECKETT DID
NOT WISH TO INCLUDE 'ONE DEAD OF NIGHT' IN THE *COLLECTED POEMS 1930 – 1978.*

FOR THE MOMENT, at seventy his own health appeared to be on an "even keel in the crooked last straight, there's metaphors for you". Yet he worried incessantly about his physical deterioration; he had an enlargement of the prostate, for instance, and, although tests showed that the condition was benign, the deaths of his friends inevitably focussed his attention on the grim truth of Psalm 90.*

His sadness spilled over into numerous little poems called 'Mirlitonnades' that he wrote mostly in 1977 and 1978. He described them himself as "gloomy French doggerel", even gloomier than his translations of Chamfort. But some of them are beautifully crafted. These *rimailles*, 'rhymeries' or 'versicules', as he first labelled them, were jotted down at odd moments in Ussy, in a hotel room or in a bar in Paris, Stuttgart or Tangier on any handy scrap of paper, envelope, beer mat, or, in one case, a Johnnie Walker Black Label whisky label. They were then often carefully reworked, before being copied into a tiny leather-bound *sottisier* or commonplace book that he carried around in his jacket pocket.

Some of the poems arose out of particular moments or incidents in his life. "Ne manquez pas à Tanger / le cimetière Saint-André" (Do not miss in Tangier / the Saint-André cemetery) with its bench dedicated "to the memory of Arthur Keyser" was composed on the first of May in Tangier, following a visit to the cemetery there. And, on a second visit to the same cemetery in August, he spotted the tombstone of a perpetual optimist: 'Caroline Hay Taylor' ("one who never turned her back but / marched breast forward", read the headstone) who had died in Ireland forty-five years before in August 1932. A parallel 'Mirlitonnade', "Ne manquez pas à Stuttgart / la longue Rue Neckar", along which Beckett tramped so often and where he sometimes ate in a small Italian restaurant, was written in Stuttgart on the day he began to direct ... *but the clouds* ..., the second television play in the Süddeutscher Rundfunk programme,

Schatten (*Shades*).** This poem is heavily ironic, for the long Rue Neckar in Stuttgart is the kind of dreary, uninspiring city road that, in Klaus Herm's words, "makes one feel positively homesick".

Other little poems were prompted by lines or phrases that had stuck in his mind during his reading: lines from Voltaire's poem about the Lisbon earthquake of 1 November 1755 (All Saints Day), for instance, or Pascal's "I seek only to know my own nothingness". Another adopts the phraseology of La Fontaine's sombre fable, 'Le Lièvre et les Grenouilles' ('The Hare and the Frogs') – he had first read La Fontaine at Trinity College, Dublin – taking its parenthetical line "Que faire en un gîte à moins que l'on ne songe" (what can one do in a den but dream) and making it the focus of a quatrain about a buck-hare ("a bouquin") that leaves its 'gîte'.

In March–April 1977, he thought of perhaps writing a play about the Fates: "Attempts to get going on something new in vain. Just a few rhymes in French. Wish I could do an Atropos all in black, with her scissors". Instead, these thoughts inspired two of the 'Mirlitonnades'. In the first, one of the Fates spins out life's thread on her spindle; in the second, the "noire soeur qui es aux enfers" (black sister who art in hell) waits to cut it; "qu'est-ce que tu attends" (what are you waiting for), he asks in his final line. The apparent slightness and playfulness of form of these late 1970s 'poèmes courts' (miniature poems) should not disguise the seriousness and, to use Beckett's own word, "gloom" of their themes. Although they have been largely ignored by critics writing about Beckett's work, they offer startling insights into the darkness of his private moods at this time.

*   *   *

Although often depressed, he continued to commit himself well into the future. Planning ahead helped to keep him going. He accepted commitments to direct the two television plays with Süddeutscher Rundfunk and *Spiel* (*Play*) with the Schiller-

* "The days of our years are three score years and ten ..."
** *Shades* was the title under which Süddeutscher Rundfunk later gathered the television plays.

Theater, and also thought of directing the French translation of *Footfalls* in Paris with the enchanting Delphine Seyrig as May. He even contemplated with pleasure a future prospect of directing Billie Whitelaw in *Happy Days*; "no harm looking forward" was his muted comment.

Beckett went to Stuttgart to direct his two new television plays in May 1977. He stayed at the Park Hotel at 21 Villastrasse, in room 422. "The hotel is not bad", he wrote, "but the room tiny. Outside the studios I see no one. In London the hotel was a sanctuary. It's not the same here. So I drag myself around the parks". In fact, he became good friends with the American cameraman, Jim Lewis, as well as the producer, Dr Müller-Freienfels. And he had known Klaus Herm, the actor in *Ghost Trio* and *...but the clouds...*, for twelve years already, having worked with him on the two Schiller-Theater *Godot* productions. As in Berlin, he visited the Staatsgalerie at quiet moments, buying postcards such as Rembrandt's painting of the Apostle Paul or a Salomon van Ruysdael to send to Avigdor Arikha and Jocelyn Herbert. But he also wrote three little poems in the Park Hotel, including one of seventeen lines, dated "S [Stuttgart] 26. 6. 77", which he gave to Jim Lewis. This begins:

> one dead of night
> in the dead still
> he looked up
> from his book.

This poem looks forward to two of his works from the 1980s, one in theatre and one in prose, *Ohio Impromptu* and *Stirrings Still*.***

*** Jérôme Lindon, Beckett's literary executor, claims it also foretells *Nacht und Träume* (1982).

SAMUEL BECKETT
ONE DEAD OF NIGHT

one dead of night
in the dead still
he looked up
from his book

from that dark
to pore on other dark

till afar
taper faint
the eyes

in the dead still

till afar
his book as by
a hand not his
a hand on his
faintly closed

for good or ill

for good and ill

S. 26.6.77

The Ghost of Youth

TIM KENDALL ON THE UNKNOWN POEMS ELIOT WAS WRITING ALONGSIDE *PRUFROCK*

T. S. ELIOT
Inventions of the March Hare:
Poems 1909–1917
ed. Christopher Ricks,
Faber, £30.00,
ISBN 0 571 17895 2

"YOU WILL FIND a great many sets of verse which [. . .] never ought to be printed, and in putting them in your hands, I beg you fervently to keep them to yourself and see that they never are printed". Despite this pleading, Eliot would have known when he sold the notebook titled *Inventions of the March Hare* to John Quinn in 1922 that his actions almost guaranteed its eventual publication. After all, a really determined poet makes a bonfire.

Although he stopped short of destroying them, Eliot considered the poems unsatisfactory. This should not obscure their importance, both for the insight they offer into the crucial years leading up to *Prufrock and Other Observations*, and because inferior Eliot is still more interesting than most poets' best work. Unfortunately, Christopher Ricks's over-enthusiastic editing seems to betray a concern that the poems cannot withstand the glare without considerable support. Generating two hundred pages of notes from rather less than seventy pages of new work, Ricks gambles spectacularly on the non-specialist reader's patience.

Nor do the poems need this kind of coddling. Many are frail devices which get trampled by all the academic machinery. Take, for example, 'In the Department Store', probably written during 1915:

The lady of the porcelain department
Smiles at the world through a set of false teeth.
She is business-like and keeps a pencil in her hair

But behind her sharpened eyes take flight
The summer evenings in the park
And heated nights in second story dance halls.

Man's life is powerless and brief and dark
It is not possible for me to make her happy.

That concluding couplet is an admission of poetic as much as emotional defeat: emptied of inspiration,

Eliot takes a rather perfunctory bow. Nevertheless, the preceding lines contain some wonderful touches: "porcelain" leads analogically to false teeth, and how much more poignant that the lady smiles "through" them than with them; her eyes and not her pencil are "sharpened"; nights rather than dance halls are "heated". It is not in Ricks's editorial brief to illuminate these little pleasures, but his obsession with sources actually distracts and detracts from them. Ricks is a brilliant critic; his collection of essays *The Force of Poetry* remains a model for academic criticism. However, as an editor he struggles with one overwhelming handicap: he's far too clever, even for an allusive poet like Eliot. Ricks's mind is one vast concordance of literature from *Beowulf* to Geoffrey Hill. Consequently everything reminds him of something else. The eight lines of 'In the Department Store', for instance, spawn over four pages of small print. Having already explained that he never draws attention to mere coincidence, Ricks locates in the poem's unobtrusive opening line – "The lady of the porcelain department" – sources as diverse as Whistler, Henry James, Longfellow, Théophile Gautier, Judith Gautier, Stuart Merrill, André Salmon, Ezra Pound and a couple of Eliot's earlier poems. This is not an extreme example. Too many notes chase their tail with a stunning but utterly pointless aplomb.

Isolated from its proper context, *Inventions of the March Hare* might seem like juvenilia. But 'The Love Song of J. Alfred Prufrock', written in 1910–11, pre-dates most of the unpublished pieces, and occurs in the notebook along with other works which fundamentally shaped our century's poetic development: 'Portrait of a Lady', 'Preludes', 'Rhapsody on a Windy Night' and so on. Ricks pushes these poems into an appendix, but ought perhaps to have retained them in their appropriate order, especially since they contain many variations on published versions. Ricks also assigns to a separate appendix what he calls Eliot's "scabrous exuberances": 'The Triumph of Bullshit' (complete with hearty chorus "For Christ's sake stick it up your ass"), 'Ballade pour la grosse Lulu', and the Columbo and Bolo poems. Eliot's vigorously scatological humour is evidently an integral, if little-seen, aspect of his imagination:

One day Columbo and the queen
They fell into a quarrel
Columbo showed his disrespect
By farting in a barrel.
The queen she called him horse's ass
And "dirty Spanish loafer"
They terminated the affair
By fucking on the sofa.

Eliot tore out such pages presumably to protect Quinn's sensibilities, removing anything in the process which happened to be on the reverse: sometimes the conclusions of poems, in one case an entire poem. Ricks is surely wrong to reinstate only the non-scabrous material. Unlike Quinn, the modern reader does not need to be shielded from poems containing what Wyndham Lewis characterized as "Words ending in -Uck, -Unt and -Ugger".

Despite these quibbles, the appearance for the first time of work by quite probably the greatest poet of the twentieth century must be cause for celebration. Admittedly, this new material seems a less important discovery than the *Waste Land* manuscript (given to Quinn as a gift, and also found among his papers), and there is nothing to match a masterpiece like 'The Death of St. Narcissus'. But it is difficult not to be excited by 'Prufrock's Pervigilium', a thirty-eight line middle section for 'The Love Song of J. Alfred Prufrock' written in 1912 and apparently rejected by Eliot not long after. This Prufrock is the creation of a poet attracted to the slums because "the contemplation of the horrid or sordid or digusting by an artist, is the necessary and negative aspect of the impulse toward the pursuit of beauty". 'Prufrock's Pervigilium' constitutes an enthralling portrait of a mind on the verge of disintegration, hearing its own madness chatter as it senses, all

around, the intangible threat of urban life.

Even the more minor poems carry some felicity, some mark of genius, to strike an authentic note amidst the Laforguean pastiche. Occasionally the reader needs to persevere. 'Paysage Triste', for example, begins with calamitous syntax – "The girl who mounted in the omnibus / The rainy day" – and hardly improves when Eliot packs the lines with monosyllables: "We could not have had her in the box with us / She would not have known how to sit, or what to wear". Then the focus switches to the silly poet and his silly companion, who know exactly how the privileged should behave in opera boxes. The lower-class girl would not

Have leaned as you did, your
    elbow on my knees
To prod impetuously with
    your fan
The smiling stripling with
    the pink soaped face
Who had your opera-glasses
    in his care.

"The smiling stripling with the pink soaped face" – a crushing self-portrait and terrific line, which deserved a better fate than to be left languishing in 'Paysage Triste'. Eliot's persona returns to his box in 'Opera', where he resists the emotional paroxysms of *Tristan und Isolde*, and begins to feel "like the ghost of youth / At the undertakers' ball". Young Possum may seem alienated by the extremities of Romanticism, but he is obviously taking notes – witness book 1 of *The Waste Land*, which quotes from Wagner's opera. And this note-taking alerts us to what is perhaps the most valuable way we can appreciate *Inventions of the March Hare*: as hints half guessed, gifts half understood, prophesying infinitely greater glories to come.

Tim Kendall edits *Thumbscrew*. His study of Paul Muldoon's poetry, published by Seren, is reviewed on p. 61.

Agog with Foam

ADAM THORPE REDISCOVERS "THE SACRAL SALT-CAKED WORLD" OF BASIL BUNTING

BASIL BUNTING
Complete Poems
Oxford Poets, £10.99,
ISBN 0 19 282282 9

Sharp Study & Long Toil:
Basil Bunting Special Issue
Durham University Journal, £10.00,
ISBN 0012 7280

MODERNIST POETRY IS MADDENING: I returned to Basil Bunting straight from A. E. Housman and for a short time found, to my confusion and dismay, the verse wrung dry of feeling as well as hard to read rhythmically. Housman's verse is tortured, yet proceeds from A to B along its lyrical, metrical vector; it works something out, even if that something is deeply pessimistic. You can carry each poem away with you like a special pebble: it knows where it begins and ends, there is cause and effect. But a Bunting poem is a spread of shored fragments – or "paratactic", as Peter Quartermain puts it in his revealing essay in *Sharp Study and Long Toil*: "Aristotle attacked parataxis, saying it strung notions together like beads on a string: parataxis places clauses side by side: equivalent value". Now there's a definition of modernism! Instead of special pebbles in the pocket, it's more like looking at the shingle from on high, with a good pair of binoculars. The end, the focus, is sacrificed to the relationships between the elements, and these elements are not hierarchically sorted – they can be zoomed in and out at will. So in this difficult century's most "difficult" poetry, the spirit of demos lurks: MacDiarmid's "Scots", David Jones' Cockney, Eliot's slang, Bunting's Northumbrian "thumps" – only Eliot is snooty towards his brilliant demotic. Modernist poets bring down the gods and heroes as they cherish their meanings: in Bunting's *The Well of Lycopolis* (1935), Venus is reduced to a gin-toting prostitute past her prime, like Eliot's vulgarised Cleopatra:

> Infamous poetry, abject love,
> Aeolus' hand under her frock
> this morning. This afternoon
> Ocean licking her privities.

This is the classical cosmopolitanism of those filled with school Latin and Greek: its cheek has been earned (unlike some recent versions of Ovid). It has always belonged to the dog-days of things – but Bunting, the much-travelled and multi-lingual son of a miners' doctor, was no Poundian authoritarian nor an iconoclast like the American Louis Zukovsky. Instead, he was a revisionist pastoralist, almost Morris-like in his championing of the local – and the tiny, wild, wind-battered stretch of Northern Europe in which he was born becomes his creative measure. His Northumbria is a very different thing from Housman's Shropshire – which Housman never knew intimately. Housman uses Shropshire as a potent pastoral setting for his poems of loss and regret, interiorising its woods and hills. As Tony Lopez points out in *Sharp Study*, Bunting uses Northumbria in a radical new version of Englishness – as a salty, northern-braced pastoral opposed to "metropolitan corruption" in the form of his London counterparts (particularly Eliot), journalism, and centralised authority in general. He was not nearly as political as Hugh MacDiarmid, and nowhere as religious as David Jones, which is possibly why he was (and perhaps still is) the neglected one of this neglected triumvirate. But his inspiration is determinedly localised in the place of his birth and, like Jones's, draws on oddball figures from the Dark Ages like St Cuthbert, perched with the gulls on Farne Isle, off Lindisfarne. Bunting is not eccentric in his celebration of this place, or that person: it is only owing to such northern monastic fastnesses that Western civilisation survived the collapse of the Roman Empire – and there were precious few of them. High on my reading list for potential converts to modernism would be Henry Mayr-Harting's *The Coming of Christianity to Anglo-Saxon England*.

Bunting's Northumbrian championing extends to the very form of his work: in an interview with the late Eric Mottram, Bunting agrees that the complex visual and verbal interweavings of the Lindisfarne Gospels were a basis for his own patternings in *Briggflatts*. But unlike those cold and lonely monks, and very like his furiously-modern mentor Ezra Pound, Bunting was as much a smasher as a builder; free with the scissors and apparently arbitrary with the paste, he gives succour to those who think of modernism as "just the same, but with the easy bits cut out". Difficulty is élitist, yes; Bunting is a poet's, even an academic's, poet. But, as Bunting himself pointed out, this is only because we expect certain things from poetry. We are like the actor who wants a line changed in a play because "I can't say it". This is hypotactic, not paratactic: the text is subordinated to the actor's ego, the mountain has to move to Mahomet. Modernist poetry stays put – "There are the Alps, fools!" as Bunting said of Pound's *Cantos*. If *we* go to *them*, we surprise and extend ourselves, and not just the view. For Bunting's chief desire, like other modernists (even late Eliot),

Basil Bunting in Tenerife in the 30s

was to discard a way of perceiving and thinking that had ended up thigh-deep in the corrupt mud of the trenches. In this early poem from the *First Book of Odes*, Bunting lovingly articulates this post-war desire:

Empty vast days built in the waste memory seem a
                                                   jail for
thoughts grown stale in the mind, tardy of birth,
                                   rank and inflexible:
love and slow selfpraise, even grief's cogency, all
                                            emotions
timetamed whimper and shame changes the past
                          brought to no utterance.

Ten or ten thousand, does it much signify, Helen,
                                        how we
date fantasmal events, London or Troy? Let
                                  Polyhymnia
strong with cadence multiply song, voices enmeshed
                                       by music
respond bringing the savour of our sadness or delight
                                           again.

Poetry here is something that breaks us out of the prison of time: landscape can so easily be reduced to mud, and emotions to an Eliotic "whimper". Most of Bunting's poetry is in praise of an early spring-

time of love and happiness: the first line is often a sappy leap off the page ("Brag, sweet tenor bull" from *Briggflatts*, or "Swirl sleeping in the waterfall!" from *Chomei at Toyama*) leaving a sexual, priapic scent. They tend to end plangently but in a "resurrection" of that springtime – like the "sweet tenor bull" descanting over the plucked river-notes of the lute in the madrigals Bunting likened to his own verse, with its enmeshings and interplays of pure sound and solid sense. Regret for lost love, lost youth, is what most lyric poems are really about, of course; poetry is the only form short enough to remember the beginning at the end. But the paratactical opening of *Briggflatts* strings a grave-tapping stonemason, densely physical and vivid particularities of Northumbrian landscape and weather, rest and graft, and the ancient kings of York, Dublin and Orkney, to make us weave love and loss tightly together as that very weave itself is set down in Bunting's invincible stone, far from the "soft slate" of the mason. It's exhilarating to experience, once you're there.

Briggflatts is not, in the end, a difficult poem. It moves from spring to winter, from Northumbria to Italy, from stonemason through legendary or mythical heroes to the poet himself, watching starlight above Farne Isle, commenting on the shepherds, refusing to fish, or steer a boat; above all, it moves from youth to age ("fifty years" more of it). So what makes it *seem* difficult? Much mention is made in *Sharp Study* of Bunting's boiling-down of numerous drafts; his schoolboy habit of cutting out "unnecessary" words from Shakespeare's Sonnets was never lost to him. He cut down *Briggflatts* from 20,000 to 700 words. We know what Pound's scissorings did to *The Waste Land*: yes, it makes the thought difficult to follow, but the result affects one in a very different way from a poem by Housman or Hardy or a Bunting contemporary like MacNeice. The great modernist poems rummage very deep indeed – in the places where emotions no longer bear names or faces, but belong to the vivid and deeply creative paratactic realm where we spend some eight hours of the twenty-four.

Housman or Hardy or MacNeice or even the "difficult" Auden can make one cry; I know of no poem by MacDiarmid or Jones or Bunting that does that. They disperse their personalities into enormous, muscling dream-currents of history and language and thought and belief; theirs is epic poetry, shell-pocked, soiled and maimed by the twentieth century. Their chief inheritor is Geoffrey Hill, and he moves me, but never to tears.

But there is nothing abstract about them, either. Like Braque's collages, their poems are made up of very real bits of the world. Bunting was a self-confessed pantheist Quaker; he is as attentive and accurate towards the concrete world as the Chinese and Persian poets he admired and imitated. When Housman lays a hand on a warm stone bridge, we are amazed by its sudden presence. Bunting's poems, by contrast, are all thinginess; yet not in the manner of, say, Seamus Heaney. Heaney, following Shakespeare's example, surprises us with a metaphoric boldness that rinses the world of its staleness. Phew, you think, I wish I'd thought of that! Few of Bunting's images renew the world in this way; they merely find the apposite word, the verb or noun or qualifier that best enacts the knottiness or smoothness or foaminess or whatever. Drystone simple is the following famous moment from *Briggflatts*:

> Rain stops, sacks
> steam in the sun, they sit up.
> Copper-wire moustache,
> sea-reflecting eyes
> and Baltic plainsong speech
> declare: By such rocks
> men killed Bloodaxe.

There's a pun on "plainsong" there: modernist art is not difficult because it has difficult parts – it's the way those parts are put together, and the odd joins and layerings they make, that have us fretting. On the other hand, even later Auden is frequently difficult because his intellect is so determined a player; with him, it's little to do with leaving things out,

> *Bunting was as much a smasher as a builder; free with the scissors and apparently arbitrary with the paste, he gives succour to those who think of modernism as "just the same, but with the easy bits cut out".*

more to do with following the cerebral clue up scree and down dale. Bunting claimed that anyone who tried to follow the clue in *Briggflatts* was doomed to failure, not because there isn't one, but because to furrow the brow in this way is to forego exactly what's valuable in the work. (The same could be said of *Finnegan's Wake*. Joyce was another of Bunting's masters.) Modernism's odd hunger for primitivism (the enforced interpretative silence of African sculpture, for instance, that Picasso so cherished) gives rise to, and is satisfied by, this suspension of knowledge, this mesmerising of reason. One could read a Bunting poem at a funeral, but it wouldn't be as unsettling, or as unbearably moving, as Housman's (or Auden's) cerebrally-passionate clarity. Bunting's poems, with their gritty vocabulary, self-hewn metres and foregoing of the usual ration of definite and indefinite pronouns, call attention to their art in a way that induces something aesthetically, more than emotionally, moving.

That is, I suppose, why the extraordinary grace and boldness of *Briggflatts* or its neglected precursor, *The Spoils*, or many of the less celebrated poems in the revised Oxford *Complete*, are as necessary to us as the poems of the *Shropshire Lad* or any of their fine successors (one thinks of Larkin's lonely gloom). The trick is not to make a polyphony out of arbitrary, discordant materials – to hang a Braque next to a Spenser, to hear Schoenberg straight after Elgar, or to read Bunting straight after Housman. The stronger the art, the more the space required around it. Bunting requires the equivalent of the Cheviots around him, their "heatherbrown flanks and white cap": he wants us "agog with foam". Like Jones, he demands the mysterious otherness of the Dark Ages, the sacral salt-caked world of St Cuthbert. This is woven by his words, but it takes time. Bunting's Northumberland is not on the same island as Housman's Malvern Hills. This is why one can cherish them equally.

Adam Thorpe's third novel and third book of poetry are both due to be published by Cape in the near future.

Camp's Out

IAN GREGSON CHARTS THE PROGRESS OF GAY WIT IN ASHBERY'S POETRY

JOHN ASHBERY
Can You Hear, Bird

Carcanet, £9.95,
ISBN 1 85754224 X

I'M INCREASINGLY BOTHERED by the gender politics behind John Ashbery's poems.

It's clear that at the start of his career Ashbery was writing in opposition to the American poetic establishment, which was aggressively masculine and heterosexual. The early Robert Lowell, for example, had an exaggeratedly virile technique: he tyrannised his material by obsessively man-handling it through rhyme, heavy alliteration, compulsive punning, into hard sinewy shapes.

By contrast, and like his friend in the New York school Frank O'Hara, Ashbery evolved a technique and language which could express his gay sensibility. Much of what was involved in this can be defined by reference to notions of "camp" and its version of irony and wit. Some of the best moments of recent Ashbery have been his most explicitly camp ones – in *Can You Hear, Bird*, for example, there is 'Sleepers Awake', where he discusses famous authors in terms of their (imagined) sleeping habits:

> Kafka, of course, never slept, even while not writing
> or on bank holidays.
> No one knows too much about George Eliot's
> writing habits – my guess is she would sleep a few
> minutes, wake up and write something, then pop
> back to sleep again.
> Lew Wallace's forty winks came, incredibly, during
> the chariot race in *Ben Hur*.

When Ashbery was starting his career, his articulation of a camp sensibility in poetry was very important, not just in literary but political terms. His use of its self-conscious aestheticism and theatricality revealed the extent to which the establishment poetic was specifically a gendered poetic, how a straight masculine perspective had imposed itself as an unquestioned norm. His work, combined with that of women poets – especially of explicit feminists like Adrienne Rich – was of great importance for the culture generally because it drew attention not just to the aesthetic expressions of gender, but its ideological expressions. This has been one of the most important and positive achievements of postmodernist subversions of monolithic "commonsense" attitudes. Its impact has been to help towards a changing understanding of how the wide range of masculinities and femininities shape each person's experience and view of the world.

It's been said that camp was postmodernism *avant la lettre*, and certainly Wilde's *The Importance of Being Earnest* has elements of parody and nihilism that now look postmodernist. Both camp and postmodernist texts employ playfulness in dealing with serious and painful issues. As Christopher Isherwood has written:

> You thought it meant a swishy little boy with perox-ided hair ... pretending to be Marlene Dietrich ... What I mean by camp is something much more fundamental ... You can't camp about something you don't take seriously. You're not making fun of it; you're making fun out of it. You're expressing what's basically serious to you in terms of fun and artifice and elegance. Baroque art is largely camp about religion. The ballet is camp about love.

One of Ashbery's greatest achievements has been his reassessment of poetic modernism through camp parody. Some of his finest recent moments have also done this, as in 'Tuesday Evening', the long poem in quatrains at the heart of *Can You Hear, Bird*:

> Such are the passwords that tired Aeneas
> wept for outside the potting shed, when,
> face pressed to the pane, he sought Linnaeus'
> sage advice. And the farm turned over a new leaf
> instead.

This reads a bit like Pound's 'Hugh Selwyn Mauberley' – the satirical juxtaposing, in a 20th century setting, of an epic hero and a giant of the Enlightenment (conveniently half-rhyming with each other) suggests a wry anti-humanist ruefulness about the loss of such potential in the modern period. But the textual references are pushed parod-ically too far, so that the stanza seems to try also to make a point about pastoral and/or Romantic nature poetry culminating in a pun that links nature and text ("new leaf"). Then again "passwords" suggests a thriller or – more likely, because of the potting shed, Enid Blyton, and "sage" is a very silly pun indeed.

This is fun. And Ashbery's been especially good at subverting the poetry of "angst" by surreally introducing trivial, or merely aesthetic things to be anxious about, as in the first stanza of his new book:

> A loose and dispiriting
> wind took over from the grinding of traffic.
> Clouds from the distillery
> blotted out the sky. Ocarina sales plummeted.

Ashbery's emphasis on fun was refreshing at the start of his career and it's still a point worth making that poems don't have to be anxious. In 'The Problem of Anxiety' he refers to the things he's "carefully left out: / descriptions of pain, and sex, and how shiftily people behave toward each other". But reading page after camp page I started to long for the things he'd left out and to find this same ironic gesture repeated so often very stale.

The fact that Ashbery has made camp boring is disturbing because it's not just a question of writing dull poems – it means he's turned what was previ-ously a subversive gesture into a predictable one. So instead of making his readers rethink their outlook he is now reassuring them, lulling them with what increasingly looks like flippancy. What started as a kind of polyphony has become monotonous, like listening to someone who always sounds sarcastic. The gender implications of this are disquieting, especially because the culture has changed since Ashbery first started doing this – camp has been thoroughly absorbed into popular culture, which it often mimicked to begin with but where its effects are often conservative. The fact that the most famous contemporary gay poet deploys a tactic that now looks like a refusal ever to speak directly or deal straightforwardly with felt experience has the effect of trivialising gays, of insinuating the idea that gays are evasive and frivolous. Camp was a bril-liant device for self-advertising, for letting straight culture know that gays were around and were a sophisticated cultural and ideological force, but straight culture no longer needs telling that. There are serious contemporary issues for poetry to deal with and which will require all its irony and wit in combination with other qualities – and this makes Ashbery's tired jokiness all the more exasperating.

Ian Gregson teaches at the University of Wales, Bangor; his critical book, *Contemporary Poetry and Postmodernism: Dialogue and Estrangement*, is reviewed on p. 5.

TWO POEMS BY JOHN ASHBERY
OUTSIDE MY WINDOW THE JAPANESE . . .

Outside my window the Japanese driving range
shivers in its mesh veils, skinny bride
of soon-to-be spring, ravenous, rapturous. Why is it here?
A puzzle. And what was it doing before, then? An earlier
puzzle. I like the way it wraps itself
in not-quite wind –
                sure enough,
the time is up. What else do you have in your hand?
Open your hand, please. Her elder seraph
just woke up, is banging the coffee-pot lid
into place. See! The coffee flows
crazily to its nest, the doldrums are awake,
jumping up and down on tiptoe, night-blindness ended.

And from where you stand,
how many possible equations does it spell out?

My hair's just snoring back.
The coprophagic earth yields another of its
minute reasons, turns to a quivering mush,
recovers, staggers to its feet, touches the sky
with its yardstick, walks back to the place of received,
enthusiastic entities. Another year ... And if we had known last spring
what the buildings knew then, what defeat, it would have turned to mud
all the same in us, waved us down the escalator,
past the counter with free samples of fudge, to where the hostess stands.
This was never my idea, shards, she says. This
is where the anonymous donors carved their initials in my book,
to be a puzzle for jaycees to come, as a nesting-ground
is to an island. Oh, we'd waddle
often, there, stepping in and out of the boat
as though nobody knew what time it was, or cared
which lid the horizon was. We'd get to know
each other in time, and till then it was all a camp meeting, hail
fellow well met, and the barstools
reflected the ceiling's gummy polish, to the starboard
where purple kings sit, and it was too late for today,
the newspapers had already been printed, telling their tale
along avenues, husks of driftwood
washed ashore again and again, speechless, spun out of control
as a pelican eyes a crater. What a gorgeous
sunset, cigarette case, how telling
the coiled rope is modeled, what perfume
in that sound of thunder, invisible! And you wonder
why I came back? Perhaps *this* will refresh your memory,
skateboard, roller skates, the binomial theorem picked out in
brutish, swabbed gasps. All the way to the escape clause
he kept insisting he'd done nothing wrong, and then – pouf! – it was
curtains for him and us, excepting these shards
of our perpetual remainder, reminder
of all those days to come, and those others, so far back
in the mothering past.

ALIVE AT EVERY PASSAGE

Roll up your sleeves,
                       another day has ended. I am not a part of the vine
that was going to put me through school
but instead got sidetracked and wandered over the brink of an abyss
while we were having a good time
in full view of the nearest mountains. *Mon tresor*, she said, this is where I
disappear for a few moments, I want you to be brave.
Sure, nothing like a date in bed,
waking after midnight to the blank TV screen
that wants us all to listen to its cute life and someday understand
what rhomboids the earth took
on its way down to get us,
that we must be happy and sad forever after. No I don't think
it was in your best interests nor do I shave with an old-fashioned straight-edged razor,
you dolt. But I was coming to that,
doing the mystifying. So if he says not to be aloha, not again,
dear me in this old-fashioned bar, however will the runts learn from their again imploded
hair balls how straight everything is.

The rest, as they say, as they say, is history:
I captured a barracuda, it was midnight in the old steeple, the clans casually
moved on us, leggings barely jerked out of the ditch. It was a folly,
to be noticed, then, astir on the perhaps more urgent
surface of what becomes one, indeed comes to become one
through impossible rain and the sly glee of mirrored xylophones.
Say only it was one for the books,
and we, we did belong, though not to anything anybody'd recognize
as civil, or even territory. I need to subscribe,
now, history will carry me along and as gently leave me
here, in the cave, the enormous well-being
of which we may not speak.

MIROSLAV HOLUB
ELEMENTARY SCHOOL FIELD TRIP TO THE DINOSAUR EXHIBIT

Jurassic
roar.

Answered by
St. Georges
or Rambos.

Only one
glum little boy,
evidently blind.
is lifted to the Triceratops
to breathlessly run his hand
up and down the skull,
over the bony collar,
the horns above the eyes,
the skin-folds on the neck,

the boy's face
is insanely blank,
but the hand already knows
that nothing is in the mind
that hasn't been in the senses,
that giants are pinkish-gray
like Handel's Concerto Grosso
that life is just a step aside
just like mother
always said.

Triceratops,
Abel's younger brother.

Dark in there, in
the midbrain:
the last dinosaur
meeting the last man.

TRANSLATED BY DAVID YOUNG
AND THE AUTHOR

SELIMA HILL
WHY I LEFT YOU

When you had quite finished
dragging me across your bed
like a band of swaggering late-night removal men
dragging a piano
the size and shape of the United States of America
across a tent,
I left the room,
and slipped out into the garden
where I gulped down whole mouthfuls of delicious aeroplanes
that taxied down my throat
still wrapped in sky
with rows of naked women in their bellies
telling me to go,
and I went,
and that's why I did it,
and everything told me so –
tracks that I knew the meaning of
like the tracks of a wolf
wolf-hunters know the exact colour of
by the tracks of the tracks alone.
You get a feeling for it.
You stand in the garden at night
with blood getting crisp on your thighs
and feel the stars spiralling right down
out of the sky into your ears,
burrowing inside your ears
like drip-fed needles saying
Get out. Now.
By "you" I mean me.
One of us had to.
It stank.

Adding to the stock of available reality…

STEPHEN BURT ON THE L=A=N=G=U=A=G=E POETS

FACTS FIRST: 'LANGUAGE POETRY' and 'language writing' describe a loosely-bounded, often hard-to-read body of work which began on the American West Coast in the early 1970s. The labels namecheck Bruce Andrews and Charles Bernstein's theory-and-criticism journal *L=A=N=G=U=A=G=E*; the poetry appeared in journals and books from then-tiny presses, some now well-known – Roof, This, The Figures, Burning Deck, Sun & Moon. An incomplete list of affiliates might include Andrews, Bernstein, Bob Perelman, Rae Armantrout, Lyn Hejinian, Barrett Watten, Ron Silliman, Leslie Scalapino, Susan Howe, Ray DiPalma, Kathleen Fraser, and dozens of other writers still active. Their declared ancestors included Gertrude Stein, Pound, Williams, Charles Olson, George Oppen, Louis Zukofsky, John Ashbery, Jack Spicer, and the New American Poets of the early-'60s war of the anthologies; their enemies included the confessional lyric, the "readerly" language of novels and newspapers, and, sometimes, capitalism.

"A neutral description of language writing", Bob Perelman states, in *The Marginalization of Poetry*, "might attempt to draw a line around a range of writing that was (sometimes) nonreferential, (occasionally) polysyntactic, (at times) programmatic in construction, (often) politically committed, (in places) theoretically inclined, and that enacted a critique of the literary I (in some cases)". Earlier books about Language writing (a good one is Marjorie Perloff's *Radical Artifice*) often focused on the movement's shared goals; Perelman's inviting history-cum-defence describes individual works and shows how widely Language writers' styles differed. It also sports a verse-essay prologue and epilogues more fun, and more enlightening, than some of the poems it describes:

In language writing any president of any body may name a cloud a whale a whale a cloud a whale a whale a cloud a cloud. If so, she should be complimented, complemented, and called on it.

To appreciate, to be changed by, a given piece of Language writing should not necessarily require that we buy into any of the movement's ideologies, just as we should not have to be Christians to be changed by a poem of George Herbert's. But arguments about individual works of Language writing can turn quickly into arguments about interpretation in general, since the political contingency of meaning and value are what many of the poems are *about*. Bernstein's 'A Defense of Poetry' ("My problem with deploying a term liek / nonelen / in these cases is acutually similar to / your / cirtique of the term ideolpigical / unalmlsing . . ." – spellings his) is, Perelman writes, in its non- or anti-sense "an attack on all evaluative judgements . . . grades, awards, tenure, the canon could not exist in a regime where language was composed of singular nonhierarchical marks – if such could be called a language . . ."

Like most polemical literary movements, the Language writers set themselves large-scale, confrontational, political, critical goals: they wanted to overturn older ways to read. Perelman: "The new sentence . . . is defiantly unpoetic. Its shifts break up attempts at the natural reading of universal, authentic statements; instead they encourage attention to the act of writing and to the writer's multiple and mediated positions within larger social frames". Perelman presents these aims as descriptions: *here is what one kind of poet has been trying to do to you* (and, if she succeeds, she may change how you read other kinds). But these objectives can come across as demands implicitly made on all poets, as in Bernstein's fascinating, frustrating *A Poetics* (1992); Bernstein calls for work which "destroy[s] . . . not meaning but various utilitarian & / essentialist ideas about meaning" and he and other advocates of Language writing sometimes sound as if poets who left "ideas about meaning" intact were all headed for the dustbin of postmodern history. The best response to claims of that sort is what Alan Jenkins (not the poet) wrote in *How to be in a pop group*:

All great music is experimental [. . .] Experimental music may involve building some new instruments the like of which the world has never seen using such elements as four hundred feet of steel tubing, some weasels and a mountain, and then using them to play a piece of music written in special notation invented for the purpose which incorporates a new three-dimensional eighth-tone scale; but on the other hand it may involve having the backing singers go 'doo' instead of 'baa' during the chorus of 'Teenager in love' to see if it sounds any better.

'Language writing' as a self-conscious movement is, Perelman argues, over, but its adherents continue to write in ways that reflect its founding ideas. Bernstein's most interesting recent poems can be read as verse-essays whose slangy word salads include bitter humour:

> ... Poetry services provide cost savings
> to readers, such
> as avoiding hospitalizations (you're less likely
> to get in an accident if you're home reading poems),
>   minimizing
> wasted time (*condensare*), and reducing
>   adverse idea
>   interactions
>
> (studies show higher levels of resistance to double-bind political programming among those who read 7.7 poems or more each week).
>   ('Lives of the Toll Takers')

Sometimes one unearths lines as good as these:

> Suspension bridges like so many
> drummers at bat, swatting flies in
> the hot Carolina sun. No, son, it
> wasn't like that – we only learned we
> had to be proud not what's worth taking
> pride in.
>   ('Locks without Doors')

– an insight into social class I'd remember no matter where I read it. But since this is disjunctive, oppositional poetics, the insight doesn't *go* anywhere; the poem scrambles away. And most of *Dark City* sounds roughly like this:

> Looking for society
> in a lamppost will not necessarily eliminate
> need for empirical
> evidence. There are the
> below-the-surface conduits
> to consider. As a rule, I keep
> my mittens in the drawer. Structure
> is metaphorical, function metonymic ...
>   ('Debris of Shock / Shock of Debris')

The problem is not that writing like this isn't interesting, or musical (it can be); it's just that a little of it goes a long way, and a steady diet of programmatic disjunction is as dull as a steady diet of anything. 'Heart in My Eye' ("Motion rises, sustains a / predilection in askance / who periodize location, slush / / boat to chimes / slow emotion...") trudges on for 97 lines, and seems designed to make us exclaim, with Gertrude Stein, "English or please english or please or please...". It undermines meaning, refuses closure, problematises the speaking voice, and forces the reader to participate in making meaning, but what else does it do? And why, once such a poem exists, would we want another like it? Readers of new poetry who also care about the poets of the past do want new styles; but we also want poems which call us back to them. We want poetry to "add to the stock of available reality" (R. P. Blackmur), and calling that desire an effect of consumer capitalism will not make it go away. I know several brilliant people who enjoy Bernstein more than Heaney; but they are not reading Bernstein for the same reasons I read Heaney, Wyatt, or Herbert. It will be said that the goals and definitions of poetry change from age to age as radically as its styles do: this may be, and yet Heaney and Wyatt and the Pound of *Cathay* have some aspects in common, aspects 'Heart in My Eye' doesn't share, and if those qualities are why we read poetry we may be ready to reject the whole enterprise called Language writing as *incompatible with* what lyric from Sappho to Heaney can give us.

But we shouldn't reject it all. The real surprise of any radical stylistic shift should be its successes, and the weirdest thing about the Language movement is that its projects and those of lyric are not *always* incompatible: some Language writers also happen to be very good (difficult) poets, full stop – to name three: Michael Palmer, Lyn Hejinian and Rae Armantrout. Palmer's first books predate $L=A=N=G=U=A=G=E$, the journal, by almost a decade (though his best work began when it did); his poems join Language-y techniques – self-interruptions, self-reference, uncertain referents – to older ones. Palmer's best writing can't be pinned down, *and* is musically captivating: it "privileges the signifier" *and* it has its closes; it confuses the hell out of us, *and* it shows us a psyche in action. Here is a favourite from Palmer's new book:

> Our errors at zero: milk for mist, grin
> for limbs, mouths for name – or else hours

of barks, stammerings and vanishings, nods
along a path of dissolving ice. The sign

we make for "same as"
before whatever steps and walls,

shutters flapping in the lighted body
called null or called vocative. I'd wanted to ask

about dews, habits of poplar, carousel,
dreamless wealth, nets, embers

and folds, the sailing ship 'Desire'
with its racks and bars

just now setting out. This
question to spell itself. And the waves of us

following what follows,
retelling ourselves

what we say we've said
in this tongue which will pass.

(Letters to Zanzotto, 'Letter 3')

The poem slips and slides among scenes it can relate only by verbal resemblance: one of its subjects is the mental life of puns. How can we imagine that we share our views of the world with other people, when such sharings may be at best accidental, slipped-into (as on ice) or sought in vain (as in a lost ship)? More local pleasures, like the puns on 0 (zero) and "O" (as in "O wind!"), along with longer ones, await.

Hejinian was central to the original Language group, publishing chapbooks and writing polemical essays. Her prose (see 'The Rejection of Closure', now in the forest-felling *Norton Anthology Of Postmodern Poetry*) can help us read her poems: if she admires Andrews' 'fx fn wlcjplofmy' (="It is proverbial") in ways I never will, she also notes her own desire "to prevent [her] work from disintegrating into its separate parts, scattering sentence-rubble haphazardly on the waste heap". In Hejinian's prose poems, especially the book-length *My Life*, mathematical arrangements, jump-cuts and programmatic disjunction coexist with accomplished lyricism: in the sense in which *Ulysses* replaces or implies, a realist novel about Bloom & co., *My Life*'s 45 45-sentence segments (one for each of Hejinian's 45 years) imply a sweetly imagistic, Woolfian autobiography. It opens:

A moment yellow, just as four years later, when my father returned home from the war, the moment of greeting him, as he stood at the bottom of the stairs, younger, thinner than when he had left, was purple – though moments are no longer so colored. Somewhere, in the background, rooms share a pattern of small roses. Pretty is as pretty does. In certain families, the meaning of necessity is at one with the sentiment of prenecessity. The better things were gathered in a pen.

The pattern is discontinuous, open; but each sentence also evokes or means something insightful, about infancy, or family, on its own, and the result is a book that, for all its resistance to closure and coherence, seems to end too soon.

Finally, there is Rae Armantrout, whose halting self-conscious ellipses of poems fold the sympathetic reader into their pared-down scenes. Her music is a bit like Creeley's, and – though she is no Muldoon – her coy shifts of topic and diction can remind me of his. Armantrout's tonal specialities include the tersely furtive, the demotically defiant, the self-cancellingly careful: her details, like her 'I', have the sadness of parts, like the isolated noses, ears and cornices in a sketchbook. Here is her 'Leaving':

The urge to wander is
displayed
in a spate of slick,
heart-shaped leaves.

*

Cellophane grass and
foil eggs.
                    The modesty
of standard presentation
does remind me of home
sickness.

*

As if some furtive
will's receded
leaving meaning
in its place:

a row of coastal
chalets.

*

With waves
shine slides over
shine like skin's

what sections
same from same.

*

Coarse splay
of bamboo
from the gullies,
I write,
as if I'd been expecting
folds of lace.

*

Mine was about
escaping Death though
Death was stylized, somehow
even stylish. So was I!
So I was hidden
among fashionable allies.

Armantrout goes on holiday, a Quest, among plant life first fertile, like hearts, then as constructed and disappointing as life at home. The sameness of cellophane and foil (or is their artificiality praise-worthy?) is like the flat sameness of a holiday beach; both convey diminished expectations, and the stacked euphonies of "shine", "slide", "same", symmetries like the succession of waves, are too formal-feeling, too pretty, to be anything but a game of solitaire, a lame compensation for not having "found oneself in nature – but what was the poet expecting to have found in nature anyway, "folds of lace"? And how can poems remedy our "urge to wander" anyway, if words are just arbitrary, referenceless signs? They can distract us; they can (with Hejinian) reanimate the world even while showing how far apart and estranging the rules of language are; and they can create new styles in which to conceal reality, and then describe their self-concealment. That last seems to me to be what Armantrout's last stanza is – coyly, tersely – doing. Here, among her fashionable nonreferential allies, is a furtive, resilient, significant poet. *Made to Seem* will not be for everyone, but its recalcitrant beauties are real, and would not have happened if $L=A=N=G=U=A=G=E$ and its supporters had not done something worth doing, and new.

Bibliography

Bob Perelman, *The Marginalization of Poetry: Language Writing and Literary History*, Princeton University Press, 1996, £13.95 ISBN 0 691 02138 4
Rae Armantrout, *Made to Seem*, Sun & Moon, 1995
Charles Bernstein, *Dark City*, Sun & Moon, 1994
Lyn Hejinian, *My Life*, Sun & Moon Classics, 1987
Michael Palmer, *At Passages*, New Directions, 1995

A ok

by Michael Heller

The Objectivists

ed. Andrew McAllister,
Bloodaxe, £8.95,
ISBN 1 85224 341 4

THE OBJECTIVIST POETS, as Andrew McAllister points out in his useful introduction to this anthology, were but briefly an organised group in the history of modernist literature. McAllister, focusing on the work of the late 1920s through the early 1940s, brackets what might be named the 'Objectivist' period in contemporary American poetry. As such, this collection provides an excellent platform or launch pad into what that poetry is about, leaving aside the later, more extensive work of some of the poets gathered here, patches of which were published in England by now defunct presses such as Fulcrum and Trigram. Recently, Pig Press brought out a good selection of Lorine Niedecker's work, and Cloud Marauder has published George Oppen. Louis Zukofsky, originally published by Cape, is now available in University of California editions of his work.

The term 'Objectivist' was the product of a contingency, coined reluctantly by Louis Zukofsky for the February 1931 issue of Harriet Monroe's influential magazine, *Poetry*. Monroe, hectored and cajoled by Ezra Pound into letting Zukofsky edit a section of the magazine, insisted that Zukofsky present his selections as a "movement" and give it a name. Along with the label, Zukofsky penned a statement, 'An Objective', less a manifesto than an honour code of a poetics, a sort of rhetorical tent under which some twenty poets were gathered. And though the label 'Objectivist' adhered to only a handful of the original twenty, the exigency of that occasion proved rather durable. Interest in the Objectivists in America and in England, as this anthology testifies, has never been higher.

What bound these poets together? McAllister limns a sociology of shared concerns, left-wing politics, religious and philosophical affinities, but also a resistance to certain aspects of the modernist project. William Carlos Williams, one of the group's forebears and senior statesmen, captures the direction the poets were heading toward in his contemporaneous remark on Pound's work, that "the principal move in imaginative writing today is that away from the word as symbol toward the word as reality". Against the decay into decor or mannerism of such modernist movements as Imagism, Zukofsky was proposing in 'An Objective' an oppositional set of terms such as "sincerity" and "objectification", critical markers and guides to poetic practice aimed at restoring a truth value to poetry that had been lost in Imagism's decline. One reads in this vocabulary a shift from literary concerns to the epistemological and phenomenological, a yearning for, as Hugh Kenner put it in describing Objectivist poetry, "no more myths".

George Oppen's early 'Discrete Series', nearly procedural in its tracking of the eye's registering of detail, is a textbook example of Objectivist poetics:

> Closed car – closed in glass –
> At the curb,
> Unapplied and empty:
> A thing among others
> Over which clouds pass and the
> > alteration of lighting

Where Imagism posed a conceit (T. E. Hulme's "moon like a red-faced farmer", for instance), Oppen's construction is haunting, strict in detail and refusing any sentimentality or false lyricism, invoking the dread and emptiness of material things, of materialism itself.

The other poets gathered here are not quite as austere as Oppen. But to one degree or another, they adhere to the suggestiveness of Zukofsky's theorising. Reznikoff, upon whom Zukofsky originally modelled the idea of an Objectivist poet, mordantly observes the urban scene or interpolates the dry language of the legal brief into his work, seeking

always, as he wrote in his poem 'Autobiography', "to use words for their daylight meaning". Rakosi, perhaps the wittiest of the group, reworks the Objectivist aesthetic in his poetry, often creating comic and deflationary juxtapositions of closely observed detail with snatches of American speech. Niedecker, who corresponded with Zukofsky for much of her writing life, is, in these pages, a powerful miniaturist, keenly attentive, as Zukofsky was, to the properties of sound and intonation. Her poems, like Zukofsky's early work, are hard crystalline gems of tonal values and condensation.

Interestingly, Zukofsky, as a poet, fits least well into his own scheme. Some work compresses the Objectivist idea of the poem, like '#20' from *Anew*, into a beautiful lyric node:

> The lines of this new song are nothing
> But a tune making the nothing full
> Stonelike become more hard than silent
> The tune's image holding in the line.

But most often, Zukofsky plays supremely literary games as in 'Poem Beginning "The"' reprinted here, which puns and free-associates its way through the Western canon, shoring, comically, at least as many fragments against ruin as Eliot. The poem anticipates Zukofsky's major work, 'A', fifty years in the writing, which enjambs into its vast length enormous amounts of literature, history, autobiography and philosophy.

From a purist's viewpoint one might quibble with the inclusions of Rukeyser and Rexroth, both fine poets, the former on the grounds of being entirely too rhetorical for the austerities of the Objectivist program, the latter for the implicit symbolism of so much of the work included here.

Still, this is a very fine and exciting anthology. The Objectivists left a permanent mark on American poetry, one which at this moment is the subject of intense debate among younger poets and scholars. To a certain extent, that debate also has its participants in England. With this collection, McAllister has brought the conversation virtually wholesale into a discourse of poetry in the United Kingdom. For that, poets and readers ought to be especially grateful.

Michael Heller is a poet and critic. His critical work, *Conviction's Net of Branches* (Southern Illinois University Press, 1985) was the first study of the Objectivist poets. *Wordflow: New and Selected Poems, 1970–1995* is forthcoming from Talisman House in the Spring of 1997.

K. M. DERSLEY
DISTEMPER ON THE PSYCHE

That Saturday night he threw away
the useless lottery ticket of life
and, without a clothes peg
against the sewer musk,
took off for the estuary.

Down the trail he powdered,
the cool resonances good to the soul of him.
Telling himself he gave not a shit
and hardly cared for man or god.
No one, not the doorkeeper at County Hall,
that ancient idiot who always insisted
on seeing his badge, had jurisdiction.
You went through life
mercifully ignoring the lot of them:
all there was to fear was fear itself.

His first love four years his senior,
that famed "Lady Inaccessible"
divorced now from the other man,
when he went to call on her
she gave him a light lunch
and showed him the door.

He sang his weird
and the goddesses of the foam
could well have listened.

Yet there are those who quibble
about an epic treatment of the housing estate,
forgetting that Troy itself
would just have been two stops round
on a 6A bus.

JOHN HARTLEY WILLIAMS
WRAPPING IT UP

Then I wd become, in my own person, America
Till everything is like Hollywood, circa 1921
Black & white, not quite threaded on the sprocket
Going imperfectly thru the gate
So a white strip zig-zags from left to right
And the piano-player, drunk on cigar-smoke
Is unable to play for the lightning that jogs his elbow

Then the world wd be my world, an odour of beer
And sawdust & men in wide hats, chairs tipped back
And actresses removing their clamourless clothes
On a regular contract to undress three times a year
Thru a haze of cheroots that has not been censored
And the imagination is in in the hands of the uninitiated
Making up the story as they go along

What I'm waiting for is the final moment
When, thru technical mishap, as always
The final frames jam & repeat themselves against the lamp
Causing a stain of melancholy to spread across the print
And light to pass transparently thru solid bodies
Reproducing an infinitely violent & humiliating surrender
To some acned mafioso in braces

The End over & over *The End*
Is written across them. She's pressed back against
The Packard convertible, three hoods watching, with guns
While the boss in white gloves stretches himself
Over her scream, & it judders & jumps in again
And a body slithers lifeless to the tarmac
Whose homicidal climax I terminate with a switch

ROY FISHER
AT THE GRAVE OF ASA BENVENISTE

with Fleur Adcock and for Agneta Falk

Churchyard woman coming quickly from under the wall:
You're looking for Plath. No question-mark.

No short way out of it but
follow the finger, stand
for a spell in the standing-place,

be seen, then duck off sidelong
to where under your stone
you're remarked on less:

Asa, translucent Jew,
your eyebrows arched
so high as to hold
nothing excluded that might want in,

it's proper to come your way,
by deflection. Exquisite poet,
exquisite – will the language say this? –

publisher; not paid-up for a burial
with the Jews, nor wanting
to have your bones burned,
ground up and thrown, you're here

in the churchyard annexe, somebody's
hilltop field walled round, a place
like the vegetable garden of an old asylum,

lowered from the drizzle in the hour between
service and wake, inventions that made life
stand up on end and shake. The church

cleared for the People Show's
deepest dignities, *Kaddish*
by Bernard Stone, alternate
cries striking the nave in brass –

Nuttall from the floor, from the rafters
Miles Davis. Your house filled up fast with stricken
friends muttering mischiefs up the stair

to the room where latterly
you'd lived mostly by the windows,

looking out, letting in, surrounded
by what used to be the bookshop stock,
priced up safe against buyers: *I can't have*
anyone taking my good friends away from me.

Afloat on the mood all day, Judi,
doing your looking-out for you
for a spell. From the middle of the room
to the window and through it, steadily
up towards Bell House Moor. Downstairs,

barrelhouse music and booze. On. Everybody.
Freed to be with you in your house again, the clocks
seriously unhitched. And visible in the crush
through the dark afternoon, Ken Smith, white
suit worn at a rakish angle, the face worn
lightly if at all. And on we go.

The stone's as you asked for it:

FOOLISH ENOUGH TO HAVE BEEN A POET,

Asa,

your hat's in the bathroom.

DAVID HART
ROOM

(In the Mark Rothko room at the Tate Gallery)

Who enters here does not enter.
Who prays here aloud stays silent.

The walls echo back no presence.
Light-of-Light storms illuminate nowhere.

I need somewhere to stay, I can't wander for ever,
if I can find a home I can be a person.

A file on the elegant shovelling in and out of personality
is opened and closed, opened and closed.

I can't feel what I can't feel in this no-space,
the walls smell of a far away land in which to wander.

The strong ship arrives but with no cargo, no hold,
no frame, no length, no weight.

If I can find a home I can be a person.
Time carries me on whether I like it or not.

The blast of the trumpet pursuing me
was never a sound only a hole in the sky

The dumb, lonely scream of the heart
claims and disowns sight.

Time carries me on whether I like it or not,
home clutches my heart, I need somewhere to stray.

This I-assuming fragment asks, Will there be grainy,
felicitous, radiant, richly paradoxical music?

Home clutches my heart, I need somewhere to stray,
I can't stray for ever, I need somewhere to rest.

Seraphic thugs from inner space
demand protection money: flesh, flesh, flesh.

The teacher's heart is cold in its box.
I need somewhere to stay, I can't wander for ever.

This I-assuming fragment fumbles to explain its terrible
invisible bright longing and the thugs spit.

I can't rest for ever, I need somewhere to wander,
straying and resting blur, bleed, bleed, blur.

This district the world, roofless hall of memory
spills the red of bleed, the grey of blur, the blue of drift.

Time continues to float the me I happen to be.
I don't know what I don't know in this no-mind.

This fiercely floodlit shed with the vaulting blown off
spills the red of bleed, the grey of blur, the blue of drift.

The angel of homecoming hovers, hovers and waits.
I need somewhere to wander, I can't rest for ever.

HELEN KIDD
CAPYBARITONE

"It is important to have your feet firmly planted on the ground
before jumping into the air" – Joan Miro

Part 1
Rabbit Discourses

I was leading fifteen Americans in bunny suits
and reading aloud, "I am the ghost of Father
Wimsatt's beard", and that was part of this poem
by Fran, could even be this poem really, and then

I was awoken by the moon, as it knocked its
light against my window like a mercury ball
wanting to cure my tooth. It danced and shimmered
its Miro memory up beyond the striggling hills just

like "The Dialogue of Insects" or "People in the Night
Guided by the Phosphorescent Tracks of Snails", and
dawn's sleeves fell back against the soft sound of the
sun that raised its arms towards the tent-maker
of the day; towards the trainee swifts that stitch
the light. And here's the ghost of a sleep song.
The poem tunes itself as, "without you I lean into
the air waiting . . ."
>   reeds in water
>   reeds in wind
ghost of an unread page
violin spook in a dusty case.

Part 2
Harlequin Carnival

It's all yours really, played in a box whose
candle is the sun, round which we phantom
figures come and go.

Giggle sandwiches for Lucy;
Robert's rabbits;
Vicki still searching for St. Horse
whose manicured hooves we faintly hear
approaching to the sound of
Emma's emu clarinet squeaks.

It was the moon's knocking made this
>   magic shadow
>   magic tree
under which, in a dream, humming "my goodness
gracious queen", we ran up to the flowers
and confronted them with hundreds of
>   terrible jokes
>   crystal bottoms
>   flying lumps
It's all Miro's imaginings for you;
"The Birth of the World", "A Bird Pursues
a Bee and a Kiss". "People Magnetised by Stars
Walking on the Music of a Furrowed Landscape",
under the light of the moon's tall ship

and my midnight paper shoes.

Magazines Roundup No. 8

fragmente; Parataxis; Angel Exhaust; Purge

by Keith Jebb

Fragmente

THE TERMS 'RADICAL' and 'avant-garde', although perhaps still the most common terms to describe the bulk of white, non-mainstream poetry in this country, are perhaps not the most useful descriptions possible. An essay by editor Anthony Mellors in *fragmente* ('Out of the American Tree: Language Writing and the Politics of Form') recalls Peter Bürger's point that the avant-garde movement of the early part of the century existed in the context of a specific historical and political moment. To try and extend those strategies beyond that moment is, so the argument goes, to produce a belated neo-avant-garde, whose productions, far from being an affront to the aesthetic ideologies of the time, have already had a cultural and economic space prepared for them. So we have a doubled question: on the usefulness of the term *avant-garde*; and on the continued possibility of the avant-garde *as such*.

The context of Mellors's essay is a discussion of American Language poetry, a movement associated with writers such as Charles Bernstein, Steve McCaffrey, Ron Silliman, Lyn Hejinian and Susan Howe. To explain Language poetry in a sentence would be pretty much impossible, but one major aspect of the theory is a form of Marxist critique of signification, the basis being the idea that consumer capitalism practices a fetishism of the signified, the consumerised sense-unit, the transferable, marketable artefact within language. The subversive practices of Language poetry foreground the signifier, the material aspect of language, breaking up what might be called the economic exchange of meaning. A bit like opening a shop that sells the customer anything they don't ask for, or, given that one of the major strategies of this poetic is the pun, like opening a butcher's shop that sells only butchers.

What Mellors accuses this poetics of is a kind of double-standard he sees in any belated avant-garde; that it claims both an innate challenge to authority (artistic and political) whilst at the same time relying upon that authority (calling itself poetry; calling itself political poetry) in order that it be interpreted (openly) (but inevitably) *in a certain way*, denying

> the possibility that the phonemic salad on the page might actually be received as being utterly resistant to meaning or simply insignificant instead of being realized as possessing the motility of what McCaffrey calls a "politics beyond politics".

It is a point worth making, as is D. S. Marriott's point in another essay from *fragmente*, 'Signs Taken for Signifiers: Language Writing, Fetishism and Disavowal'. He accuses Language writing of merely replacing the capitalist fetishism of the signified with a fetishism of the signifier. And as for their stance against the primacy of speech over writing, motivated by the notion that the fetishism of the signified is rooted in the immediacy of speech and distilled in Robert Grenier's phrase "I hate speech", he has this reply:

> Marginalized voices – black women and men writers for example, have traditionally had their claims to representation, the position of performativity, silenced, ignored, and oppressed. Grenier's dismissal of speech has a different ring entirely if one's speech has not been a privileged source of positionality and individuation but has been the source of an agonized attempt to make oneself HEARD.

This is a telling criticism, but it misses something. The very oppression he speaks of has been conducted under the aegis of, under the overwhelming and unquestioned ideology of "free speech". It is enshrined in the American constitution; it is paternalistically granted to the people of Great Britain; it is bolstered by race-relations laws; and it guarantees the dominion of the representatives of the many over the few. Getting HEARD has nothing to do with "free speech". A hegemony that can allow free speech is confident of its own ideological security, that it can keep marginalised voices on the margins. To get HEARD is to utilise the voices, the languages of the dominant ideologies against themselves. What neither Mellors nor Marriott mention with regard to Language writing is its resort to punning and parody. Far from being simply a fetishism of the signifier, Language writing presents a continuous substitution of the unexpected for the expected. When Ronald Reagan introduced the Princess of Wales (that was) as "Princess David" he was a Language poet (albeit unwitting but that's not the point – when John Ashbery claimed the US President [was it Ford?] was a surrealist, he never meant he knew he was a surrealist). In a sense, therefore, it makes sense that the Language poets are all WASPish, the language they deconstruct is in fact the language they own.

> ... Language poetry foreground[s] the signifier, the material aspect of language, breaking up ... the economic exchange of meaning. A bit like opening a shop that sells the customer anything they don't ask for, or ... like opening a butcher's shop that sells only butchers.

The fact that *fragmente* publishes essays like this which are not couched as reviews is something to be glad of. It is also something which links many of the magazines publishing radical/postmodernist poetry in this country, that there is an ongoing debate about contemporary poetics which goes on alongside the practice of writing poetry.

So broad is this debate that this issue also includes a review of Jacques Derrida's recent text, *Aporias*. As for the poetry itself, Bob Perelman's 'The Manchurian Candidate: A remake' is a fine long poem from which quotation won't do justice. One of the (sadly only) two women in the issue, Sheila E. Murphy, gets the prize for best first line, "She signed up for blushing lessons" ("Pansies white around the inner red"), and I like this from John Welch:

A body is all hollows, bow
Stretched in the air, air
Is an absence waiting

It is the shape I
Hollow here in my region
Of silences but you knowing

Me: [...]

('Poems')

I like Harriet Torlo's lapidary short lines too. Nich-

olas Piombino (poet and psychoanalyst) gets eclipsed by George Hartley's medley essay 'Silence from Babel: on Nick Piombino', which makes me wish there had been enough Piombino to live up to it.

Parataxis

issue 7 is a special issue devoted to 'Original: Chinese Language-Poetry Group'. Edited by J. H. Prynne, with translations by Jeff Twitchell, it is a glimpse into a very important contemporary nexus of aesthetics and politics. The Originals are a group of six poets (5 men, 1 woman) born between the mid-fifties and mid-sixties, and mostly connected to Nanjing University. Most of the poetry in this selection is by the two leading members of the group, Che Qianzi and Zhou Yaping. It is the latter, in his prose 'letter to j. h. prynne' who gives the clearest expression of the group's motivations:

In China the usual accusation against us is:
cutting apart ideology and art. Those precocious
and sophisticated political critics, as long as they
cannot determine the meanings of characters and
phrases in our poetry with their limited thinking,
will assert that our ideas are obscure, game-like
and playful. This is more or less like saying that
if the lines they desired were not realised by Klee
or Miró, they will criticise them for being simple,
childish, and meaningless.

If this makes Chinese critics sound a little like Mellors and Marriott, it may not be entirely fortuitous. The Originals are very interested in and knowledgeable about twentieth century Western literature and art – names like Robbe-Grillet, Barthes, Pound, Tzara are used as touchstones, especially by Zhou Yaping – and although the Language poets themselves do not get discussed here, there is the sense of an independent but parallel development:

In our poetry, language becomes the purpose itself,
rather than a mere tool, simple or complex. This is
the new excitement brought to poetry by language.

We are no longer in the mood to rename the world,
our attention is focused on the materialised capabili-
ties of language itself (not something behind language)
(Huang Fan, 'poetry's new shore: language')

This may not be what we would expect (or *want* to
expect) from post-Tiananmen Square Chinese radicalism. The potted biographies of these poets show
that all have been denied official publication for at
least some of their work (a few early volumes of less
radical verse seem to be the exceptions), and all are
subject to a high degree of critical censure for playing
"language games". But they have not met the labour-
camp silencing of other more directly oppositional
voices, and far from being a compromise, this is a
strength. A strategy which means they get HEARD:

It must be pointed out that the language experiments we are pursuing, after much passionate labour,
have been welcomed by a fairly large circle. Not by
the authorities, on the contrary by the freedom and
choice of those friends who are even younger than
ourselves.

(Zhou Yaping, 'letter to j. h. prynne')

It is tempting to confuse Language-based writing of any kind with abstraction. But to subvert the
"realities" language encodes takes a firm grasp on
those realities, not the avoidance of them. Take this
from Che Qianzi's 'fictitious fish':

Collect one 'fish' character after another
– The fish of writing is too abstract
It arranges them into the shape of a fish
A straw rain cape, but without flesh
The fish of writing melts into the face of the water
    The fish of writing
Is blown away by a breeze
An icy straw rain cape without flesh coming
A straw rain cape but without flesh

Or this from Zhou Yaping's 'apples and art, 25
poems':

10. (A poster: at Nanjing University)
An American astronaut
Was written in a notice with white chalk
An American astronaut
Was notified of this sort of chalk
White
That is
'An American Astronaut'

More amazing
Than all the amazement he has ever known

All of this demands of course a note on the translation, Jeff Twitchell's impossible task of rendering
the ideogram in the phonetic, aided by a team of
women from Nanjing University, who apparently
produced the original draft translations. What has
been achieved is a series of texts which remarkably
avoid the "exotic" affect of much translated Chinese
poetry, as Prynne puts it in his 'afterword': "to them
we are the exotics".

Angel Exhaust

13 'Poetry and Socialism' includes a long series of
essays by various hands on the history of Left poetry
in Britain during the twentieth century. If I run
into my reservations first and lament the perfunctory treatment of feminism by Andrew Duncan,
and the fact that no woman poet is actually written
about for anything more than a sentence, I also
have to say that in many ways this is one of the best
resumés of the century I have read, even despite
this gob-smacking series of omissions. Andrew
Duncan's discussion of Charles Madge surfaces one
of the forgotten writers of the century with a
sympathetic and open-eyed treatment. Perhaps the
prominence the same writer gives to Christopher
Logue defeats me, as does his dismissal of Adrian
Mitchell, but John Wilkinson on John James in the
'70s is excellent at locating the nexus of a rather
'50s machismo with punk, in a rather effete
Cambridge atmosphere, which has left almost no
record of itself either in published volumes by
James, or in the authorised versions of the century's
poetic 'history.' It is very interesting to see W. N.
Herbert treated as a poet who emerged in the '80s.
A few pamphlets published by himself and Robert
Crawford in Scots have actually been read south of
the border, and the poet of 'Ticka Ticka Glendale'
from *Forked Tongue* is there for all to see. The Bill
Herbert who spent the Eighties in Oxford, producing samizdat mags like *Tyromachia* in English as
well as co-editing *New Poetry from Oxford*, which
gave the first half of Tom Raworth's *West Wind* its
first British publication, is a less known, but no less
interesting figure.

As you might expect there is some very good
poetry in *Angel Exhaust*, including some of the best
from Barry MacSweeney I've seen for some time
(I've probably missed a lot), and such dependable

names as Nigel Wheale, Peter Middleton and Robert Hampson. Rob MacKenzie is a very impressive discovery for me, a writer who mixes Scots and standard English and deals more in open form than the likes of Herbert and Crawford. But I'll quote MacSweeney doing a very deliberate male Sylvia Plath:

> I sit in the garden reading Homer, shy lad
> under a folding one-man tent, and daddy wants to
> murder me.
> Daddy, I caught a trout, Honest I did Dad.
> Daddy, I caught a dace away on holiday in Dorset
> and it was argent like the moon when I ran, I ran I
> ran away
> for fear of everything and you.
> ('Daddy wants to murder me')

Purge,

edited by Robert Hampson, stands at the opposite end of the spectrum, production-wise, from the A5 perfect-bound likes of *fragmente* and *Angel Exhaust*. Photocopied, using the writers' own A4 drafts (a medley of fonts, some on no-doubt trusty portable typewriters), it still manages to publish the likes of Charles Bernstein, Rosemary Waldrop and Denise Riley. We are after all in a world where money and prestige are still not more important than respect, and Robert Hampson is justifiably a very respected editor. It therefore seems more apt than an indulgence that rather than publish another issue last year he produced an 'interim edition' of his own poem *Seaport*, written during the late '70s and early '80s and tracing the rise and fall of the city of Liverpool, up to the Toxteth riots. Left unfinished, it is still good to have the text in print. The clarity of Hampson's writing is remarkable, giving us an unfussy run through some of the seminal facts and events of the city's history. As a history it is probably as effective as any text-book could ever be, adding speed of transmission, sharpness of selection and skilful juxtaposition. He shows the effectiveness of avoiding the emotive for the blunt. Emotion, after all, is the reader's reaction, and irony is the reader's observation:

> *ii. kenneth oxford decides to use police vehicles driven at*
> *speed to disperse rioters*
>
> one mans' back
> broken

> david moore (22)
> a disabled man
> visiting his sister
> killed:
> dragged along
> by a police
> "hit-&-run
> driver".

> *iii. kenneth oxford wants armoured cars*

fragmente
ed. Anthony Mellors,
Available from: Dept. of English,
University of Durham,
Elvet Riverside, New Elvet,
Durham DH1 3JT
Appears: yearly
Format: c. 120pp A5
Rates: £4.95 single issue
Reviewed: Issue 6, 1995

Parataxis
ed. Drew Milne,
Available from:
School of English and American Studies,
University of Sussex, Falmer,
Brighton BN1 9QN
Appears: irregularly
Format: c. 90pp A5
Rates: £4.00 single issue
Reviewed: No. 7, Spring 1995

Angel Exhaust
ed. Andrew Duncan,
Available from: 27 Sturton Street,
Cambridge CB1 2QG
Appears: twice yearly
Format: c. 140pp 8vo
Rates: £4.00 single issue
Reviewed: No. 13, Spring 1996

Purge
ed. Robert Hampson,
88 Ashburnham Road,
London NW10 5SE
Appears: irregularly
Format: c. 40pp A4 stapled
Rates: £2.50 single issue
Reviewed: interim ed. of Robert Hampson's *Seaport*

POETRY INTERNATIONAL

25 OCTOBER – 3 NOVEMBER

EVERY TWO YEARS POETRY INTERNATIONAL COMES TO THE SOUTH BANK,
BRINGING POETS FROM ALL OVER THE WORLD TO READ ALONGSIDE BRITISH POETS.
WE PRESENT HERE A SELECTION OF POEMS BY SOME OF THE POETS AND
ONE AMERICAN STAR REVIEWING ANOTHER – MARK DOTY ON JORIE GRAHAM –
PLUS DON PATERSON ON MARK DOTY'S NEW COLLECTION.
FOR TICKETS OR A BROCHURE CALL THE ROYAL FESTIVAL HALL: 0171 960 4242.

GEOFFREY HILL
MYSTICISM AND DEMOCRACY

Open me the gates of righteousness: That I may go into them ...

You see the terrain he has won back from but not won;
the ravaged moon is a mere cranium, a mandarin crown,
                              compared to these craters.
He is indeed a survivor and of the intolerable elect.
Enforce for jollity's sake the solemn retaking
of the earth that has been his, many times over, by deed.
Project through lanterns of hot oil the festive advance –
                    it is at once a retreat
to that furthest point where lines of vanishing converge.
The obscurities though which you have armed his way,
night marches, down-draughts of coal smoke,
                              many-chambered fog lit from within,
become to hurled applause: the Veil of the Nations, the Final
Transformation-Scene-and-Curtain, Apocalypse-Hippodrome!

Reprinted by permission of Penguin Books from Geoffrey Hill, *Canaan*.

Canaan (Penguin, £7.99, ISBN 0 14 058786 1) is Geoffrey Hill's first collection for
ten years. His translation of Ibsen's *Brand* is just published as a Penguin Classic.
Geoffrey Hill opens the festival with a reading at the Purcell Room on October 25.

TWO POEMS BY
HANS MAGNUS ENZENSBERGER

IN MEMORY OF SIR HIRAM MAXIM
(1840–1916)

I (1945)
On the way to school, in the ditch,
the roar of the fighter-plane swooping down,
little clouds of dust to the left, in front of us,
to the right, soundless, and only a moment later
the aircraft gun's hammering.
We did not appreciate his invention.

II (1854–1878)
Later, much later did he emerge
from an old cyclopedia. A country boy.
Their farm in the wilderness, harassed
by bears, a long time ago. At fourteen,
a cartwright's apprentice. Sixteen hours a day
at four dollars a month. Scraped along
as a brass-founder, boxer, instrument maker,
shouting: A chronic inventor, that's me!
Improved mousetraps and curlers
and built a pneumatic merry-go-round.
His steam aeroplane, with a boiler
of 1200 pounds, three tons water-supply,
broke down under its own dead weight.
Neither did his ersatz coffee take off.
He had to wait for the Great Paris Exhibition,
a fairy-world of arc-lamps and filaments,
for the Legion of Honour and for his illumination.

III (1881–1901)
Three years later the Prince of Wales
could inspect in the vaults of Hatton Garden
a miracle of precision:
it loaded, cocked, bolted and triggered,
opened the breech-lock, ejected the shell,
reloaded, cocked, again and again, by itself,
and the cadence was fabulous: ten rounds
per second, continuous firing.
The recoil barrel, a stroke of genius!

cried the Duke of Cambridge. Never again
will war be what it used to be!
A weapon of unprecedented elegance!
The knighthood was not long in coming.

IV (1994)

Nowadays of course, with his masterpiece
being available on any high school yard,
we fail to feel what he must have felt:
the compulsive joy of a bearded mammal
with 270 patents to his credit.
As to us, his juniors by a hundred years,
we lay low as if dead in the ditch.

ADDRESSEE UNKNOWN
– RETOUR À L'EXPÉDITEUR

Many thanks for the clouds.
Many thanks for the *Well-tempered Clavier*
and, why not, for the warm winter boots.
Many thanks for my strange brain
and for all manner of other hidden organs,
for the air, and, of course, for the claret.
Heartfelt thanks for my lighter and my desire
not running out of fuel,
as well as my regret, my deep regret.
Many thanks for the four seasons,
for the number e, for my dose of caffeine,
and, of course, for the strawberry dish
painted by Chardin, as well as for sleep,
for sleep quite especially, and,
last not least, for the beginning and the end
and the few minutes in between
fervent thanks,
not to mention the voles out there in the garden.

TRANSLATED BY THE AUTHOR

These poems are taken from *Kiosk*, by permission of Suhrkamp Verlag.

SHARON OLDS
A CHAIR BY THE FIRE

If there had been a flash fire,
that afternoon, would my parents have first
untied me, and then carried me out,
or grabbed the chair and carried it out
with me tied to it? It would have looked
odd on the sidewalk, two adults and two freestanding
children, and a child softly affixed,
a secret grandmother of the house. They did not
know how else to stop me from pouring
ink on their bed, they thought I was a little
possessed. And I do look weird, eight years
old and bound, like a nursing-home drooler,
as if the device on my backside is a kind of
walker, an anti-walker. If they had gone
out, and a flash fire had come,
I could have simply stood up, bent forward
at a right angle, wrists at hips,
formal bow of an abject subject,
an object relation, and titupped down the stairs.
That could have been done without a fire,
I could have swung against a wall
and dislodged my maple saddle, but I sat
obedient. And I almost remember
the touch of matter, for those hours, wooden
touch. If there had been a fire
that day, besides the tiny one
which gutted a back closet in my heart,
I could have done a Joan of Arc,
or been carried – tipped, here and there,
with small flames, like a late maple,
winter coming – out onto the walk
and been seen by the neighbors, Mrs. Langmaid,
Mrs. McGlenaghan, Judge MacBain –
and I might have felt like a child who had never been
allowed outside, now looking around
through my own eyes, as who I was,
seeing the curb, and the sidewalk, and the path
to the front door, and the pillar of magma
where that home had been.

JOHN TRANTER
SNOWY

Drinks, I'd had a few, Snowy said; I shouted a round
for the blokes I knew. We argued: is there a way
to expunge the influence of Ezra Pound
from modern literature? Tempers fray
when thinkers argue over rhyme, far
be it from me to drink too much tonight.
They say inspiration is insight, when they are
deluded and drunk with delight.

Another brimming cup
of brew, another snort of snow
and it's time for the thinkers and tinkers to get up
and leave the fellowship and go
from the gathering hand in hand
not caring if it shines or rains.
They grumble and mumble, but at last they stand
dutifully in line, and they catch their planes

and fly home to where the unyielding beast
of work pins them to a blackboard. Some are undersized
and disgusting, some gargantuan, some others at least
adequate physically and their tiny talents prized
by students, their meanderings inscribed in the purple dye
from an indelible pencil. Listen – in the hallway, the tread
of fame. Blood vessels at the back of the eye
or the whack marks on the back of the head –

it's all a pattern. No, you can stay
after the farewell party, please do
what you do do best, please go away
to where you
have a special friend
Snowy said,
to where learning comes to an end
and theory and example are interbred.

There's always another side
to every question, for example, Is he rough
trade? Is rough trade within his stride?
Taking the rough with the smooth, that's enough
to send a fellow to the mental home
where he may yet learn to distinguish between
the shadow and the substance. Since I first commenced to roam,
Snowy opined, I ain't seen

nothing to match that clump
of women, and the quizzical curve to that one's eyebrow –
or a garment as dazzling as that pink jump
suit your girl friend is now
not entirely wearing. Are you feeling all right?
Life's full of bumps and spills
but they say "out of sight,
out of mind", and behind the nearby hills

who knows what bird with limping wing
warbles, and haunts that special place.
What's that you're wearing? Is it a wedding ring?
And then on the pool's surface I seem to see her face
dissolving and reforming under the wind's lash
as the ripples distort the view –
Dash dot, dash dash dash
cried the bird, then away it flew –

the sunset like a coal fire, black
and red. From behind the rocks the tread
of purple thunder rolling out and churning back
into the valleys made the air thick and horrid overhead.
Take each new idea slowly, that's the way,
dream obliquely and cast your net wide
on the stream of thought, and say good-day
to the drinkers and thinkers who fall by the wayside.

Your motto – pull
over, take a deep breath,
make sure the tank's full
and laugh at death.
That's how to get ahead.
Be of good cheer.
Never waste time talking in bed
and learn to smile at fear.

He measured the book from side to side – 'twas three feet
long, and two feet wide. Getting into his stride
he flung himself into the pilot's seat
and love took him for a ride.
He left the ground
and up he went;
frightful the sound
of his swift descent.

And once more behind the low neighbouring hill
the bird warbles for a while, then is mute,
then speaks again, and the evening is finally still.
Why do you exhaust yourself in this forlorn pursuit
of knowledge? Wise men, and many, you have met,
and noted what their weary eye reveals:
that wisdom is the ticket, yet
an agitated madness dogs the heels

of those who seek it in the foam
and blather of intellectual strife. Track
wisdom to its lair, its distant home,
you'll find the journey leads you back
to where you started from. Hark to the trot
of distant steeds, the jingle of the spur –
fame tests your temper, whether it's cool or hot,
whether you're a brave lad or a cur.

You're broke? Snowy asks. You could do with a raise.
You say you're feeling low? You lack the high
that mad ambition gives. Cold? You need the blaze
of love to warm you up. See the sky?
Why is it always blue? Why do the dancers sway
to the dizzying music? They swing wide,
he said, from the narrow track of today
for the sake of the song, my boy, the reward of the ride.

The lines of this poem use the end-words of the nineteenth-century Australian
ballad 'The Man From Snowy River', a tale about a bush horseman and his
plucky steed, by A. B. Paterson.

GORAN SIMIĆ
CHRISTMAS

"I'm blind", I say. I don't speak again
for a very long time. Of course,
I'm lying about being blind: if I look
out of the window, to where
the children are singing carols, I see
how the snow seems to fetch a rainbow;
I see frozen songbirds fall
from the branches; I see a butcher haul
a slaughtered lamb down the street.

It is night. An icon burns in the stove.
There's a seamless drone from the airport
that makes me want to weep.
"I am blind", I say, "I am blind".
She doesn't say a word. She beats
the Devil's tattoo on the tabletop.

"I've forgotten", I whisper. I don't speak again
for a very long time. Of course
I'm lying about having forgotten: I think back
to hoofprints in the snow and dogs on a leash.
It was a manhunt. I remember my father laughed
when I barked at the birds.

"Have you ever noticed how a vacuum-cleaner sounds
like a plane in take-off, or how
a TV left on too long will fix a room
with a hot and heavy smell? Have you noticed
the depth of frost?" I ask her,
"Have you noticed this incredible frost at all?"
She's got nothing to say for herself.
She might not have heard.

I won't speak again. I'll sit here and watch
the traffic lights adapting endlessly
to whatever's best. That's me, I'm just like that.
A whole universe buzzes above
the control tower: isn't that strange?

Fish in the depths are strange – the way they live.
The smell of hay in an orchard
is too strange for words. Now and then,
someone winks from the bottle:
the genie, the Puck of plum brandy.
"Can you see me?" I ask. "Can you see any jot
of me, any tittle?" She nods, but of course
she's lying. As if I cared, as if
she could understand the half of what I say.

TRANSLATED BY DAVID HARSENT

RUTGER KOPLAND
THAT EVERLASTING BEAUTY

(Mondriaan)

He began in that fortuitous world, that unfathomed
confusion of lines and smaller lines which, for instance,
became a tree,

he named this beauty the tragical
beauty of the man who sees it
from moment to moment

he did not want to see how this world
passes away, but how everlasting it is
when it turns back

to that one moment when its lines
disintegrate to become a tree for instance,
to become its formula.

he died and saw everything, saw everything and died.

TRANSLATED FROM THE DUTCH BY JAMES BROCKWAY

EDWIN MORGAN
SALMON

We hung over the falls, watching.
The river groaned as the gorge narrowed,
its turmoil was white, extravagant.
All this was far below. Once through,
it was crashed on by the waterfall
in a sort of massed chaos. The splashes
were brilliant, the spray was very fine.
A rainbow dared to cross the uproar.
That was not what we came to see.
But there they were, one, two, six,
some red, hook-jawed, stacked and packed with
energies they brought from Greenland,
backs, snouts testing the spumy
half-air half-water element
they must jump through, even fly through –
they sprang, they soared, they gaped, they gasped,
lashed frantic tails, fell back, quivered,
lurched up again, making it, some,
some stunned on rocks, but a great one
first, high, and his mate soon after,
nonchalant, nudging each other over
the sexy gravel of the spawning-beds,
the cock and the hen, in their last fettle,
ecstasy of the cloud of eggs,
ecstasy of the burst of milt,
the thrust of indomitable life.

PIOTR SOMMER
APOLITICAL POEM

Nature's engine ticked, twittered, and bubbled,
hummed and rumbled, almost soared,
though the river was shallow,
small, in fact a brook,

the afternoon sun was warm,
rain wasn't falling, and crickets
changed shifts smoothly, technically perfect,
you couldn't hear the gaps, it was like

some absolutely chock-full silence:
the mechanism ran on steadily
and didn't choke at all
on itself or on the surfeit of voices as if it was still

covered by warranty
issued by who knows
whom, without stamps, without paperwork,
with words, or even with the wind,

and yet in the machinery
everything played on, rolling,
not quite so evenly, as now nearer
now further off, from all sides,

moderately or forcefully, as it
pleased, like an orchestra
whose particular ingredients, primary
elements, that is the instruments

and maybe the audience too:
the blades of grass which
my eyes embraced, nettles and ferns,
didn't move, just

stood there,
as if they were either dead or
still had time, or
patience.

TRANSLATED FROM THE POLISH BY M. KASPER
AND THE AUTHOR

Mending the Visible

MARK DOTY ASKS "WHAT OTHER POET HAS SUCH NERVE, SUCH GENUINE GRANDEUR?"

JORIE GRAHAM
The Dream of the Unified Field:
Selected Poems 1974–1994

Carcanet, £12.95,
ISBN 1 85754 225 8

IT'S ONLY IN the last few years that the word "project" has become a familiar word in the discourse of American poetry. Though I know poets who dislike it intensely – for its suggestion of wilfulness, as if a poet's concerns were something chosen – the term seems to have stuck. Perhaps because we've needed a shorthand tag for something that's in the air: an interest in the particular strategies, both in form and content, through which a poet stakes a claim on meaning and approaches that quality of unmistakability or idiosyncrasy which is the hallmark of an achieved style. What we want from poetry, I believe, is the sense of an individual sensibility engaged in negotiations with reality; how does this perceiver, this voice go about the work of making sense of the world? Such individuality is achieved usually not in single poems but in constellations of them, as we watch a set of questions played out, investigated, inhabited across time.

Whether one likes the term or no, it seems impossible to talk about Jorie Graham's work without examining her "project". Not since the late 1960s, when so many American poets (James Wright, W. S. Merwin, and Adrienne Rich among them) abandoned formalist stances for the practice of a free verse in which voice and image were considered paramount, has there been such a dramatic instance of self-reinvention. One can't read Graham without considering her continuing re-evaluation of what a poem can hold, and of the appropriate relation between poetic structure and the actions of mind, between form and consciousness. This is what makes *The Dream of a Unified Field*, such a bracing, useful book. This trim selection (197 pages culled from her five volumes) allows us to see the architectonic nature of her self-transformation all the more clearly.

Graham published two early collections, *Hybrids of Plants and of Ghosts* (1980) and *Erosion* (1983),

which established impeccable lyric credentials while also demonstrating her meditative bent. Here, clearly, was a philosophical poet, interested in the classical epistemological problems of how we know and how we say what we know. A few lines from the lovely 'I Watched a Snake' give witness:

> I'd watch
> its path of body in the grass go
> suddenly invisible
> only to reappear a little
> further on
>
> black knothead up, eyes on
> a butterfly.
> This must be perfect progress where
> movement appears
> to be a vanishing, a mending
> of the visible
>
> by the invisible . . .

A familiar movement, there, from reportage on the natural world to inference; the progression of thinking is Emersonian, as the poet looks to nature for clues to human purpose and possibility.

One has only to hold that bit of meditation about nature next to this one, a description of a blooming amaryllis from 1994's *Materialism* to catch something of the flavour of Graham's poetic evolution.

> The self-brewing of the amaryllis rising before me.
> Weeks of something's decomposing – like hearsay
> growing – into this stringent self-analysis –
> a tyranny of utter self-reflexiveness –
> its nearness to the invisible a deep fissure
> the days suck round as its frontiers trill, slur
> – a settling-ever-upward and then,
>   now,
> this utterly sound-free-though-tongued opening
> where some immortal scale is screeched –
> . . . stepping out of the casing outstretched,
>   high-heeled –
> something from underneath coaxing the packed buds
>   up . . .
> ('Opulence')

What has happened here? For one thing, the poet's lost interest in the orderly presentation of 'I Watched a Snake', in which meditation or analysis followed description; here, the "self-brewing" of the bulb is described in such a way as to render also a perceptual process, a flux of ideas, associations and metaphysical speculations. Even Graham's syntax – phrase tumbling after phrase – seems to mimic a dynamic process of thought, as if the poem were an embodiment of all the active gestures of perception which this lively examining mind brings to bear upon the object of investigation. And thus the "object" is never exactly itself, but consciousness as an agency, the transforming, connecting power of attention. In this case, a sort of storm or torrent of attention, in which language seems almost to whirl around its ostensible subject. It's no accident that one of Graham's recurrent words is *whir*. (Here one thinks of Ashbery, who says in his *Three Poems*, "The event arrives flush with its edges". Graham is interested in the edges, the linking points where one thought joins another, where perceptions combine into a flurry of verbal gestures.)

At least by implication, Graham addresses the new reach her poems will attempt in a stunning poem from *Erosion*, 'At Luca Signorelli's Resurrection of the Body'. After invoking the image, in the painting in question, of souls hurrying back to carnal form, the poet turns to Signorelli's study of anatomy, the painter's attempt to find in flesh the "vanishing point so deep / and receding / we have yet to find it, / to have it / stop us". Signorelli's desire to study the nature and depths of the flesh is so profound that, upon the death of his only son, he dissects the young man's body:

> It took him days,
> that deep
> caress, cutting,
> unfastening,
>
> until his mind
> could climb into
> the open flesh and
> mend itself.

The poem represents, I believe, an extreme example of the artist's credo: a declaration of the willingness to push deeply into experience, to go beyond (or under or behind) the surface, even when the surface is a beloved one.

"God knows I too", Graham says in a later piece,

"want the poem to continue". But the poem as we know it does not, from 1987's *The End of Beauty* on, continue. Instead Graham seems a kind of anatomist of perception, in her insistence on complexity, on mapping the precincts of thought. A multiplicity of viewpoints blur the simpler perspectives of earlier poems in service of her quest for the larger structures of meaning – much like Signorelli in search of his "vanishing point".

This will to anatomise (even if it means that the familiar or beloved surface of the world is obscured or erased) is remarkable, and it is most startling when allied with Graham's drive to address the central questions of her time. She is fundamentally a religious poet, in this most secular of hours, and she is obsessed with delineating a spiritual condition: our desire for a transcendent sense of meaning called into radical question by the Holocaust, by a century of terrifying diminishments of the human. In a period in which American poets have turned their focus toward the psychological, the personal, seeing themselves as capable of speaking only within a limited arena, Graham's ambition has been almost boundless; there are few American poets willing to address the crises in consciousness and moral life, the disastrous implications of our century's history. The fragmentation of meaning, the ruptures in continuity implied in our history extend, in her poems, to language itself, to the meaning-making function. But Graham, restless investigator, is not content merely to fragment. In her best poems (the harrowing 'From the New World' for example, which focuses on the terrible story of a girl who survived the gas chambers only to be sent back in again, and considers the impossibility, in the face of such a story, of saying what it is *like*) Graham has built a poetic architecture capacious enough to allow for an examination of our central nightmares: the failure of personal and social utopias, the breakdown of ethical foundations, the dissolution of humanism in the light of our questioning of the nature of the self. What other American poet has such nerve, such genuine grandeur? Genuine, I think, because of an odd humility; Graham's study of the urgent dilemmas of her time begins with whatever is at hand – an amaryllis blossom, the movement of leaves, a band practising in the neighbourhood park – and rises to a headlong confrontation with history. *Project* seems too slight a word for it, this work of a feeling intellect fully engaged in her moment, with its contradictions and terrors, its promise of new meanings arising out of the cracks in old ways of making sense.

Multiple Choice

by Don Paterson

MARK DOTY
Atlantis
Cape, £7.00,
ISBN 0 224 04400 1

THE FIRST THING that you have to say about *Atlantis* is that it isn't half as good as Doty's last, *My Alexandria*; those tics that were merely bothersome in the earlier volume seem to have grown fat on Doty's increasingly casual delivery. To write as if poetry were anything other than a very deliberate act seems to me an act of self-deception. By that I'm not suggesting that it should always *look* deliberate, but Doty's attempts to cover his tracks can seem highly disingenuous, which is precisely the last thing they intend. No-one would think of describing the prose style of Doty's fine memoir *Heaven's Coast* (Jonathan Cape, £16.99, ISBN 0 224 04390 0) – which movingly charts the progress of the AIDS virus in his partner Wally, and which I would recommend unreservedly – as either insincere or homespun, but what passes for naturalism in prose often ends up sounding like the old "plain folks" routine in verse. We're invited to play Doty's game of pretending that these poems are half-finished, while we know damn well that poems are finished like nothing else in the world. This is enacted, to take one example, in his habit of asking rhetorical questions; while there was a rash of them in *My Alexandria*, there is an epidemic in *Atlantis* . . . "What was it I meant to tell you?" "Toward – what?" "What is the body?" "What to call it? Lumina, aurora, aureole?" I dunno, Mark. *You* choose. It reflects that peculiarly American desire to appear to allow the reader to participate in the compositional process, and derives from a misplaced democratic instinct that perversely – in its diaryese – ends up excluding the reader. Poetry

. . . in the best of . . . [Doty's poems] . . . we are spoonfed with so much genuine love and delicacy we forgive him for treating us like a child . . . but at its worst, his relentless unpacking of all significant detail starts to feel as irritating as having your big brother unwrap your Xmas presents.

generally aspires to sound like either the first or the last word on the subject, but when it tries to sound like just the third or fourth, we can cease to care about it.

Here's an unfashionable reflection: of all poets I can think of, Doty reminds me of Heaney more than any other. Doty's obsession with the weight, texture and taste of the world, its aspiration to the platonic forms, and the business of its reduction to its irreducible qualia, is precisely Heaney's own, even if his subject matter – a technical irrelevance – is very different. For Heaney, as for Doty, the achievement of that descriptive accuracy, in its act of returning the world to us, scrubbed clean of the encrustations of habit and cliché, is of itself an act of moral restitution. For the reader, the internal validation of this accuracy comes, in Heaney's case, more slowly these days; slowly, because his ear has long outstripped our own; but the pleasure is, if anything, the keener when it arrives. Doty – here, at least – is a lot less accurate. We recognise most of his effects very quickly, because – "Iridescent, watery / prismatics: think abalone, / the wildly rainbowed mirror / of a soap bubble sphere / think sun on gasoline" ('A Display of Mackerel') – we might well have thought of them ourselves. Thus Doty, it would appear, feels the need to judge and moralise to make up the shortfall.

The trouble is that he has too few good habits in his style that would automatically legislate against the sort of descriptive excess to which he is temperamentally prone. In Doty's poems we are always spoonfed; in the best of them we are spoonfed with so much genuine love and delicacy we forgive him for treating us like a child, and acquiesce in it; but at its worst, his relentless unpacking of all significant detail starts to feel as irritating as having your big brother unwrap your Xmas presents.

Much of *Atlantis* is pastoral and meditative, and Doty cuts this in great swatches. He spends a lot of time thinking about colours. As he puts it rather beautifully ". . . my art / could only articulate the sheen, / or chronicle the fashion in which / the world gains lustre as it falls apart" ('Two Ruined Boats'). Colours are great, of course, but if the employment stems from an Adamite belief that the world can still be nailed into place, if only we can get the names right, it tends to short out the discourse of association in which most poets are continually engaged, and which Doty, on the strength of his last book, seemed better equipped than most to conduct. It isn't penetrative enough, for me, at least, merely to have observed that something is "jonquil" or "chartreuse".

Mind you, when Doty scores, he still scores pretty high: with 'In the Community Garden', sunflowers – only bloody marram grass has inspired more crap poems – for once get the poem we all knew they deserved. Yeah, we get the stuff everybody jots in the notebook – "Though some are still shining confident, others can barely hold their heads up . . ." etc . . . but the end rejects the poet's – and implicitly our own, since this is a collective conceit – sentimental animism:

Renate Pensold

> Do you think they'd want
> to bloom forever
>
> It's the trajectory they desire –
> believe me, they do
> desire, you could say they are
>
> one intent, finally,
> to be this leaping
> green, this bronze haze
>
> bending down. How could they stand
> apart from themselves
> and regret their passing . . .

'Crêpe de Chine' sounds terrific, like Sean O'Brien in drag: "Look at the secret evidence of my slip / frothing like the derelict river / where the piers used to be"; the second part of 'Fog Argument', 'Beach Roses', like all the best of Doty's poems is one, long, beautiful exhalation.

But elsewhere, Colm Toíbín's puff – "Formally perfect, with wonderful control of the stanza . . ." – rings decidedly hollow here: Doty's versification is standard pastry-cutter stuff, with little attempt at any serious argumentative or episodic definition, without which stanza becomes merely a way of making the poem more attractive to the eye. Moreover you'd hope a "formally perfect" writer would notice, for example, that the start of 'Two Cities' forms the first three lines of an almost perfect anapaestic ballad; the fact that this seems to have been entirely fortuitous depressed the hell out of me. The page exerts too little reciprocal pressure on Doty's pen. Jarrell once said "True poets, so to speak, turn down six things and take the seventh"; Doty gets to the seventh alright, but includes the other six too. The pleonasms aside, he cheerfully ruins his best effects by compounding them – "a dozen yellow-eyed minnows / thread the bright ripples / like a pack of embroidery needles / on amphetamines . . ." Most of us would've been delighted to come up with the original image, but *on amphetamines* for God's sake?

With a writer like Doty, whose subject matter is often so intrinsically moving – the book seems populated by couples, one of whom is dying – the reviewer is in an invidious position; but while I have to side with Sheenagh Pugh in the "unopened children" debate (see letters pages of past two *PR*s), like Hartley Williams I'm wearied that a poem's tear-jerking ability should be taken as a sign of its intrinsic worth. Most of us, myself included, wept copiously throughout *Kramer versus Kramer*, but could still tell it was mince. Nonetheless, you feel as if you'd turned up during the funeral to check the tilt of the tombstone and see if they got the dates right; but surely this is the only way of trying to ascertain whether or not Doty's memorials and elegies will last. There is no way of – and no point in trying to – quantifying the humanity of Doty's response to his subjects, or of our response to his poems. But we can talk about the rest, and to judge by *Atlantis*, Doty is a very uneven writer indeed.

Don Paterson's second collection will be published by Faber in 1997.

A Transit of Thom

CHRIS JONES INTERVIEWED THOM GUNN IN SAN FRANCISCO IN JULY 1995,
A FEW DAYS AFTER THE POET'S 66TH BIRTHDAY. THIS IS AN EDITED VERSION OF THE
CONVERSATION, WHICH TOOK PLACE BEFORE THE DEATH OF DONALD DAVIE.

CJ: Are you a good critic of your own poetry, I mean what sort of value judgements do you make when considering your work?

TG: I don't pretend to be an objective critic about my work. I think I can be an objective critic about anybody else's work, but hardly about myself because I know where it came from, and of course all the ideas behind it are important to me, and I have sweated over certain phrases, so I value that probably more because it means more to me. You must remember that Milton preferred *Paradise Regained* to anything else he had written because that was the most important subject.

CJ: But you do write about your own poetry.

TG: I don't evaluate my own poetry. I have written memoir-like things at times. I know what you are thinking about, you are thinking about 'Writing a Poem' in *The Occasions of Poetry*, and the autobiographical bit in the same book, but surely I haven't written in the way that critics would write.

CJ: So you have never thought of writing a book like Ted Hughes's *Poetry in the Making*?

TG: The book broadcast for children? That's an interesting book. No I haven't written like that, but that's not really about his own work is it? I mean he writes about 'The Thought Fox' as I remember but he doesn't evaluate it, he just gives his own example surely of how he came to write something. This is something any writer can do and it can be interesting, it may not be interesting always, but it can be, especially if it's a poem like 'The Thought Fox' and how he wrote that, which is something he can tell us but the critics can't tell us.

CJ: Have you got a good idea about how the processes of writing work?

TG: It varies with every poem. As you know from any poetry reading a number of questions arise afterwards – which I am not sure is such a good idea – anyway one of the questions is: 'How do you write a poem?' You don't know how you write a poem but you can recall sometimes how you came to write a specific poem and sometimes you can't recall it at all. It varies. I don't know what it depends on. If it was a particularly freaky or funny or peculiar way that you wrote a poem, you may recall it. If you take six months over it obviously you recall some of it.

CJ: Are you into rewriting poetry still?

TG: Yes, oh yes. It doesn't get easier.

CJ: Even after it's been printed in a magazine you might come back to it before it has been published in a collection?

TG: I don't usually publish in a magazine before I'm pretty sure it's finished. But I sometimes change things; quite often I just change a phrase or some punctuation or some small details, but I make alterations, yes.

CJ: At the beginning of your career there was *Fighting Terms* which went through a number of changes . . .

TG: And they were all mistakes, yeah. And now I have come back to the beginning. I learnt from that not to do it again.

CJ: Do you think the critics respond differently to you in America? I was reading the back cover of your *Collected Poems* in a book shop, the American edition, and the critics seemed to be much more positive in a way.

TG: Well, I would say the main difference is that the American critics tend not to come to me so early in my career as the English critics do. I was very lucky in my original reception in Britain, and I got praised probably rather too much for my first two books, and they got quite well known, and ever since then I've been judged in the light of those two collections. Though both of the books were published over here in tiny editions, I'm not even sure they got reviewed very much; they didn't hit people's consciousnesses, the general consciousnesses of where the critics are, and so I haven't got judged so much in relation to my beginning. They have taken my books as they came out much more on their own merits. Also the American critics have been much more tolerant (a) to the homosexual content and (b) to the free verse that I have taken on board, and to other measures like syllabics. They are much more interested in that kind of thing, whereas the English critics have tended to be more conservative both towards the subject matter and the style, the metrics.

CJ: You quite often talk about yourself in terms of being a derivative poet. Are you aware of imitating other writers when you are creating a poem?

TG: You may be more aware of my influences than I am. You don't set out to be influenced though sometimes you do, you know. Sometimes I'd like to be the twentieth century John Donne or I'd like to do an imitation of a poem by Ben Jonson. You think that kind of thing but very often you are the last person to know about the people you are really being influenced by. You think you're doing something else to the original, but that's true of all stages I think, right from the earliest poems you write:
– This is a poem all of my own!
– No it's not! W. H. Auden wrote it first of all! But you didn't realise it!

CJ: It's interesting that you should mention W. H. Auden here, because he seems to be a powerful influence in your early poetry, although not many critics have talked about that. I can think back to one of your earliest published poems, 'The Soldier', which seems to be very Audenesque really, and in *Fighting Terms* itself you use a lot of images about soldiers and spies, battles or potential battles that seem to come from an Audenesque perspective.

TG: I have a particular friend called John Mander who was another poet at Cambridge at the same time as me, and he and I used to read Auden's poems together. I was going through Auden about a year ago, I was going through the *Collected Poems* that I had at that time. I was astonished at how much was familiar to me. Yes he was a tremendous influence.

CJ: Is there the idea of camouflaging your own sexuality like Auden in your early poetry?

TG: I'm sure that came into it because it did with him too. He was doing that. I didn't realise that he was queer when I first read him. I'm not sure when I did. I mean I knew the first time I ever saw him read which was at Stanford in the mid

1950s. I knew then but I didn't know when I read him at Cambridge.

CJ: So when you first read *The Orators* you had no idea?

TG: I loved *The Orators*. I still love it actually. That's a very strange piece of work isn't it? It's wonderful, in fact it seems to me that it shows the most promising direction he could have taken, but he didn't alas!

CJ: It's interesting that even though you spent most of your years of education in England you have written a lot about American writers and not much about English writers.

TG: I'm more interested in twentieth century American poetry than I am English. I think American twentieth century poetry is more interesting than the English. It's true, there's Yeats, but he's Irish anyway, and there's Thomas Hardy, but he started in the last century. But then you get the modernists who are tremendously exciting. But what do you get going on in England? Well, you get Auden eventually.

CJ: And Bunting.

TG: Oh Bunting, he's the great man.

CJ: Another Anglo-American, like Auden.

TG: Well, he combines the two, he does something. I wish I could do it but I can't; I'm not the person to do it. He does something that's almost inconceivable. He manages to converge the twentieth century American with the English tradition. In *Briggflatts* there is both Pound and Wordsworth. Who would have thought they could both be there? It's entirely Bunting. That to me is the most exciting poem probably of the whole twentieth century.

CJ: You tackle this in your essay 'What the Slowworm Said' in *Shelf Life*, comparing his achievements to Pound's and Eliot's. I remember you writing a review in *The Yale Review* in the early 1960s which wasn't too positive about Pound's work at that time.*

TG: Yes, I wrote an essay I shouldn't have written – a review of Pound's *Thrones* which I haven't allowed to be reprinted. No, I don't think that's the good age of Pound but I shouldn't have said such a thing because the rest of Pound is so wonderful. Well in 'What the Slowworm Said', I had a tremendous admiration for that Canto [Canto 47], as you know, the *Cantos* are terrifically uneven. I hope I never read the Chinese

* 'Voices of Their Own', *The Yale Review*, 49 (Summer 1960), pp. 589–591.

Cantos again! I can make my own précis of Chinese history! But the good Pound is wonderful, the good Pound goes right up into *The Pisan Cantos* of course. But Canto 47, that's the one that originally endeared later Pound to me. I got into the *Cantos* through that and it's wonderful.

CJ: With Eliot you have been more evenly critical?

TG: I started liking *The Waste Land* much more since I wrote that essay, partly from teaching it. My students love it so much that I started to love it. It's extraordinary and original, and so much of a repellent poem. But there's nothing like it for its vigour and craziness. It's a crazy poem. Of course now we know he was having a nervous breakdown when he was writing it, so that explains it. My problem with *The Waste Land* I mean, it is a bit like Beethoven's Fifth – you hear it so often you get kind of blunted. I don't think I'd take back anything I said about Eliot in the essay but I would also say a few more good things about him. I do think there is such snobbery, which I find very repellent. It's alright for Elizabeth and Essex to have sex, and Anthony and Cleopatra, but not the young man and the stenographer you know, when they have sex it's vulgar!

CJ: In one early review you wrote, you commented on the end of the second part of 'The Waste Land', talking about Eliot "slumming in a London pub".*

TG: There is an element of slumming that I don't like about that.

CJ: It's interesting that you should begin by being so anti-modernist.

TG: That was not just myself, that was my generation.

CJ: This is what connected you with the Movement?

TG: I was just going to try to say that without using the word Movement. As you know, I don't think of myself as being a member of The Movement. But I was very much a member of my generation and we were very tired of modernism and of obscurity of that sort. God knows my early poetry was obscure, but that was ineptitude! That was me not being very good! Yes we were certainly reacting against modernism when I was an undergraduate. But then you know I came over here and read Williams and Stevens.

CJ: Was that a great changing point?

TG: Reading any modernist was a change!

CJ: But it wasn't all American poetry. I mean you reviewed Ted Hughes's *Lupercal* and one of Donald Davie's collections, and you stated then that you thought they were the best writers of their generation.**

TG: I love *Lupercal*, yeah.

CJ: There is still a sense of you liking English Poetry?

TG: Well, I kept up with my contemporaries.

CJ: There is an interesting review you did of Wallace Stevens's *Collected Poems* in a 1956 review for the *London Magazine*.***

TG: That's only interesting if you are interested in me to start with. It's not very good.

CJ: Well I think it's interesting because in the same edition, just below that piece, there's a review of Larkin's *The Less Deceived* and of a collection by Elizabeth Jennings. It's interesting that from where you are in America you should choose to write about Stevens and not about Larkin and Jennings.

TG: I loved Larkin's first book. There is a review which you probably haven't come across because it was published under a pseudonym: Apemantus, like the character in *Timon of Athens*. This is still when I was an undergraduate at Cambridge, and an anthology called *Springtime* came out. It was probably my first public appearance and it was the first I had ever seen of Larkin and they needed somebody to review this book. Since I was in it I couldn't review it under my own name. I was very funny about myself, I said: "We have seen better from Thom Gunn". I thought that was sufficiently modest. And I was saying how wonderful Larkin was and of course Larkin was wonderful. I don't think he's been a good influence on English poetry, as I have said much too often I'm sure, but his early poems were. I'm not speaking about *The North Ship* because I hadn't even read that, I didn't know it existed at the time. These were poems like 'Wedding Wind' you know. You could hardly call them Movementy poems, I mean the word Movement wasn't to be invented for some time after that. 'Wedding Wind' was

* 'Manner and Mannerism', *The Yale Review*, 50 (Autumn 1960), p. 132.
** *Poetry*, 97, no. 4 (1961), pp. 266–70.
*** 'Collected Poems' by Wallace Stevens', *London Magazine*, 3, no. 4 (April 1956), pp. 81–4.

almost Lawrentian, and he was tremendously refreshing and I continued to find him refreshing, though with less enthusiasm. At the time of his death somebody asked me to write about his poetry and I read it through and I thought what an embittered man he was.

CJ: The Bunting–Larkin thing, you tend to see that as a dichotomy almost really.

TG: Well it is. I agree absolutely with Donald Davie about this: Bunting would be a very good person to be well known by young men and women who are possibly going to turn into poets. Surely *Briggflatts* is troublesome yes, the references are troublesome, you have to look up reference books, but it's not so much to ask: the rewards are enormous. He would be a good influence on people, and unfortunately Larkin is a bad influence. Larkin is really a fine poet, it's just that the kind of things he is doing do not transfer well to other people. Whereas the kind of things you can learn from Bunting are the kind of things you can learn from Lawrence. Lawrence is tremendously exciting; he is often a good influence on people. What you have to remember is that we were all influenced by Lawrence, including the poetry, which is wonderful, and is probably still not enough liked, partly because people call him sexist. He's much more complicated than simply being a sexist. He's certainly anti-women, I mean, yes he is, but he's anti-men too! He's an exciting person taking up exciting subjects. You can see what I'm getting at when I say that Bunting and Lawrence, entirely different poets, are both good and positive influences on people, and I don't think Larkin is – he aims so low.

CJ: It seems to me that as you got older you seemed to go further back in your borrowing from modernist writers in your work.

TG: You think so in my poetry? I guess so.

CJ: Have you ever written in open form, in the way Robert Creeley or Robert Duncan would understand the term?

TG: No, not really. I revise my free verse poems just as much as I do my other poems. I write my own way you know. I get it down bit by bit. I write it either fast or slow and I'm not ashamed of revising. Of course, the impulsive first moments when you get something down are wonderfully exciting but it's not projective writing.

CJ: Even though you experiment still, your later poetry seems more assured regarding the kind of styles you employ. Personally I think *Moly, Jack Straw's Castle, The Passages of Joy* and *The Man with Night Sweats* are all very good books.

TG: You can imagine how pleased I am to hear that because *Moly* got almost unreviewed, it was certainly never liked. It took, as a collection, longest to go to paperback which means nobody was buying it, nobody liked it and the reviewers hadn't liked it. And then people were fairly kind to *Jack Straw's Castle*, although they said it wasn't as good as what came before, and then there was positive barbarity, in England anyway, with *The Passages of Joy*. But my stock immediately rose with *The Man with Night Sweats*.

CJ: They didn't like *The Passages of Joy* because of the sexual effrontery do you think?

TG: I think sexual effrontery but there's also the free verse effrontery. The English took that very badly.

CJ: In the essay on Ben Jonson in *The Occasions of Poetry* you wrote you talk about puns and how much they were valued in Jonson's time. Then you went on to say how much they are looked down upon today as if they were some sort of childish joke, and of course the title of the book is a pun ...

TG: I remember Ian Hamilton being particularly bitter about that: that was really cheap of me! I didn't think it was cheap. I thought it was funny, but there you are!

CJ: It's interesting what Donald Davie wrote about *The Passages of Joy* in his book *Under Briggflatts*. He was quite critical then, particularly about the effect of the gay content in your work.*

TG: Yes it wasn't entirely positive. I took notice and I said that since I respect him and like him as a person, and I respected that review, I wanted to prove to him that good homosexual poetry can be written. I said: this will show him – in *The Man with Night Sweats*. Certainly his view is an eccentric one. There are so many queer poets in history, Marlowe and Whitman just being two of the more famous, or Auden you know, it struck me that it was a strange view that such a project was not tenable.

CJ: He seems to associate your rejection of pre-Enlightenment writers with a dropping off in standards in your work.

* Donald Davie, *Under Briggflatts: A History of Poetry in Great Britain 1960–1988* (Manchester, 1989), pp. 171–81.

TG: Well, his point I suppose would be most fairly expressed by the fact that he thinks that homosexuality is a modern phenomenon and of course now the most recent commentaries about this speak of sexuality as a social construction, which he would have a little difficulty with. Of course it's very interesting: what do you think of Shakespeare's sonnets as being? Homosexual seems the wrong word. Yes, they are addressed passionately to a man. What did he think of himself as being, particularly as there wasn't a term for it. There was "buggery" but he's not speaking about buggery, or at least I don't think so … well there's so many sexual puns! But none the less, homosexuality as a word only has a history of about a century at most. So I suppose Davie has a point there. I took notice of Davie's review because I respect him and because it was a persuasive review, I thought, of *The Passages of Joy* and I wanted to disprove that. I wanted to show him he was wrong.

CJ: It's interesting that Gregory Woods was arguing exactly the opposite in his book *Articulate Flesh*. Whereas Davie saw your poetry at an end, Woods saw *The Passages of Joy* as a beginning.*

TG: That was a relief. I was very impressed by that book I must say as a whole. He says wonderful things about Ginsberg.

CJ: There is an epigrammatic quality to your most recent work. Why did you choose to write in that style?

TG: Anybody who worked with Yvor Winters got predisposed towards the epigram because he liked the epigram a lot. Jonson liked the epigram a lot and so I've always taken the epigram seriously and I've got a few more for my next book, whenever that comes out!

CJ: Of course there's the poem 'JVC' in *The Man with Night Sweats*.

TG: 'JVC' was one, yes: J. V. Cunningham …

CJ: He wrote many epigrams himself.

TG: Someone asked me to write something for a memorial issue of the *Chicago Review* for J. V. Cunningham. I was astonished that I could write a poem that was a kind of imitation of him.

CJ: You said the poems in part four of *The Man with Night Sweats* are a book within a book. Do you think the collection is unified?

TG: I think a lot of it is unified. I got the poems together and I knew I had a book there in 1988. I couldn't think how to arrange them and two friends helped me. My instinct is to separate free verse poems from metrical poems as you know, but one of my friends, Robert Pinsky, pointed out that's not necessary at all, and also I thought putting all the AIDS poems together would be too much but somebody, maybe Jim Powell or Robert Pinsky, suggested I put them together. I'm glad I did, it makes them a lot stronger. I have very seldom written poems as a sequence in that sense. I wrote many of those poems together because people started dying around about the same time. Though I had written the very last poem in the book, and I knew it was going to be the last poem in the book ['A Blank'], I didn't think of that as forming a group. I was going to disperse them amongst the rest of the poems which would have been a terrible idea. It would have been confusing. So I did form a book within a book. I'm pleased with it now.

CJ: You seem to be writing a lot more about your mother now, and the death of your mother …

TG: Well that was a poem waiting to be written as soon as I could write it, you mean 'The Gas Poker'?**

CJ: Yes, and then there's 'My Mother's Pride' which is a different kind of poem.***

TG: Well, I couldn't write about her until then.

CJ: Is this because you have always been against a certain kind of confessionalism, like that exhibited by Robert Lowell?

TG: I have never wanted to write like that and I guess that's why I couldn't write about my mother's suicide in an obvious way. 'The Gas Poker', well that's kind of modelled on a Hardyesque kind of poem. I was thinking in terms of a Hardy poem.

CJ: Whitman has seemed to play a big influence on your most recent reviewing, on your attitude to poetry in general.

TG: With Whitman it was a comparable kind of discovery to that of the Marianne Moore of 1925. I have always been aware of Whitman, and D. H. Lawrence has a nice essay where he quotes one or two good things by Whitman but I got terribly put off by some of his more later,

* Gregory Woods, *Articulate Flesh: Male Homo-Eroticism and Modern Poetry* (London, 1987), pp. 212–31.
** *Three Penny Review*, 49 (Spring 1992).
*** *PN Review*, 77 (January/February 1991), pp. 45–6.

public poems like 'When Lilacs Last in the Dooryard Bloom'd', which I know some people like a lot but which I really don't like that much. My revelation was with the early Whitman, which all came out with one tremendous impulse, and it is that first version, which is sometimes reprinted as a book of the 'Song of Myself' with the other early poems like 'Crossing Brooklyn Ferry' and 'The Sleepers', which have a kind of vigour and a kind of sharpness of language and imagery that he never really matched after 1860. You know Wordsworth's *Prelude* wasn't published until about 1850 and then the first collection of Whitman's was 1855; it's an enormous jump of the ego! But reading that early work by itself, it has a crispness that he really lacked mostly after 1860. But he got very unsure of himself, he got very unsure of his sexuality. He's outrageous in those early poems. I'm sure that one poem of 'Song of Myself' is really about having outdoor sex with a lot of other men on some place by the sea. It seems obvious when you realise that. But a lot of people didn't realise this about him because what people were mainly shocked about with Whitman when he first published was that he was saying that women could have as strong a sexual impulse as men, and that revolted people! It seemed obvious to him as it seems obvious to us. I needed to get through a lot of the famous later stuff and find out what I really liked to find out about Whitman.

THOM GUNN
THE PAINTER AS AN OLD MAN

Vulnerable because
naked because
his own model.

Muscled and veined, not
a bad old body
for an old man.
The face vulnerable too,
its loosened folds
huddled against
the earlier outline: beneath
the assertion of nose
still riding the ruins
you observe the down-
turned mouth: and
above it,
the assessing glare
which might be read as
I've got the goods on you
asshole and I'll expose you.

The flat palette knife
in his right hand, and
the square palette itself
held low in the other
like a shield,
he faces off
the only appearance
reality has and makes it
doubly his. He
looks into
his own eyes
or it might be yours
and his attack on the goods
repeats the riddle
or it might be
answers it:

> *Out of the eater*
> *came forth meat*
> *and out of the strong*
> *came forth sweetness.*

CLARE POLLARD

I HAVE LIVED all my life in Edgworth, near Bolton, and am at present study-ing for my A-levels at Turton High School. Next year I hope to study Literature at University. I love the Beatles, tacos, travelling, clubbing, and my friends. In my spare time I enjoy writing songs on my electric guitar and am near to completing my first novel, *Ugly Fruit*.

It was only a year ago that I started writing poems, and initially it was just clichéd teenage angst stuff, but I have improved a lot since then, encouraged by the English Department staff at my school. My main inspirations are Plath and Sexton, and I try to write poetry as emotionally charged as theirs. The prose-poetry of Elizabeth Smart's *By Grand Central Station I Sat Down and Wept* also made a great impression on me, as did the colloquial style of Ntozake Shange's choreopoem *For Colored Girls Who Have Considered Suicide When the Rainbow is Enuf*, and I have loved violent imagery ever since I read Lady Macbeth's "I have given suck..." speech. I have not been to any workshops or Arvon courses, and am entirely self-taught.

HARA-KIRI

It is as small, complex and compact
As a microchip.
(God must be Japanese.)

They will hook it out limb by limb.
Tough veined trout pink flesh
As raw as sushi.

Nothing will remain of it but
Bloodspots on her bright white sheets
Like stubborn flags.

If she let this grow it would
Cripple both of them.
Hearts mutated by the fall-out.

It would want to die for her.
Kamikaze pilot.
A noble death.

It's karaoke!
Everybody in the ward sing:
"Baby, where did our love go?"

Career prospects and finances and practicality
Are squatting like sumos on her mind,
And this rising sun holds no promise,

For she will attack herself at dawn
And there will be
No surrender.

She will slit herself open.
Watch it and her intestines slip out
In the light of a Samurai sword.

ZAGHRUDA

I try not to recall the darkest times
For fear that hate will rot away my womb
Khun mae   *mon Soeur*   daughter
Yes – we touch long desire feel ache also
Yet you branded us whores   *huren*

In the brothel the *Harem* (skirts up round our thighs)
We lay back and thought of
Kuche – centre of our world
Jollof rice dumplings *bamii nam* lasagna *basturma*
At the *suk* we purchased food for you with given coins

Sari   izar   veil   tarha
They smothered us   We saw but were not seen
Invisible people devoured by night

I heard of one Asian who killed herself
When you laughed and laughed at the meadows
Of soft dark hair on her limbs
We pasted lead on our skin to make us *bleich* for you
You liked us cripples   our feet golden lilies

No ambitions but for you master
Whilst you said come on darling sweetheart kitten
Dog *querida* sweet potato pie
In Borneo menstruating women must
Sit on the roof for 3 days

Defloration may involve a sharp stone
or a fist wrapped in cloth
And of course we love the stink of baby crap!
We want to pluck our brows until we weep   *Yed mae*
You sucked our milk then spat it in our faces

The other week Iran was on the news
Many men mutilated their own flesh for Islam
At first I cried with joy to see
They had caused themselves to suffer also
Hallelujah!   Fierce *sang rouge* dripping

Only then I saw their wounds were as deep as ours
Saw the pained desperate smiles as they tried to be strong
Three men died that day
Oh brother   *padre*   *sohn*   lover
We anoint your cuts with *yaah saneh* through choice

Forgiveness is easy between equals
Take our hand and we'll love you
Poor sad *Don Juan*
I know we can survive this together

EVERYTHING ENDS IN ICE

The day that I met you
Was the first day of sun.
I was shiny and new.
You thawed me in an hour;
Made me mute as a flower --
All good clean fun.

As I bit through peach fur
My longing for you grew.
Always knew you loved her,
Yet got grazed climbing trees
As you swarmed me like bees.
I sweated you.

Starved of sun, nothing grows,
And rain was all I got.
Watched my dreams decompose,
And lit trees doused in fuel.
You were Halloween-cruel.
You let me rot.

Now, I'm cold as a corpse.
My heart is blank with frost.
Skies are bleak as my thoughts;
And this numbness could slice
As I swallow the ice
And I am lost.

THE REVIEW PAGES

Melmoth the Wanderer

HARRY CLIFTON TAKES STOCK OF PAUL MULDOON AT THE STAGE OF
HIS NEW SELECTED AND THE FIRST CRITICAL STUDY

PAUL MULDOON
New Selected Poems 1968–1994
Faber, £7.99,
ISBN 0 571 17784 0

Kerry Slides
Gallery Press, £14.95,
ISBN 1 85235 190 X

Six Honest Serving Men
Gallery Press, £5.95,
ISBN 1 85235 168 3

TIM KENDALL
Paul Muldoon
Seren, £19.95,
ISBN 1 85411 160 4

MIDDLE AGE BEING RELATIVE, especially in poetry, one can say that three leading Irish poets of the last thirty years have come to terms with it recently in books-of-two-halves, looking backwards and forwards simultaneously. Seamus Heaney, with *Seeing Things* (1991) was first to the mark, the Janus face of that book looking back into the old, somewhat worked-out modes of Part One before breathing in the new, celebratory space of 'Squarings' in Part Two. Lately, Derek Mahon has followed suit with *The Hudson Letter* (1995), the first part a glance over the shoulder at his stanzaic past, before the second co-opts French alexandrines, the telegraphese of Hart Crane and the vision of late Kavanagh and early MacNeice into a new, expanded meditative whole. In between these two, with *The Annals of Chile* (1994) has come Paul Muldoon.

One difficulty, perhaps, with Muldoon's book-of-two-halves is that it was harder to tell which half contained the future and which the past, a confusion the poet himself perhaps shares if his re-order-ing of material from that collection in the present text is anything to go by. Rather riskily, given the success of *The Annals of Chile* and the apparent departure it represented from a ten-year period of confusion since *Quoof* (1984), Muldoon has chosen to incorporate its most accessible poems into his *New Selected*, thereby putting most of his eggs in one basket. Unsurprisingly, he stares out at us from the front cover like a rather nervous Paul McCartney asking Is There Life After the Beatles? Ahead, as so often with this poet in the past, lies *terra incognita*.

Whatever the future, the lines of the past are effectively disentangled in the first chapter of Tim Kendall's new study. The Armagh childhood, of a not untypical "mixed marriage" between the market-gardening father so warmly evoked from 'The Waking Father' to 'Cauliflowers' and the *faux-culturée* teaching mother etched, rather less charitably, in poems from 'Ma' to the recent 'Yarrow',

> She had read one volume of Proust,
> he knew the cure for farcy.
> I flitted between a hole in the hedge
> And a room in the Latin Quarter.
>
> ('The Mixed Marriage')

Subsequently, the explosive coincidence of meeting Seamus Heaney, the start of the Troubles, the years at Queens and the precocious *New Weather* published by Faber in 1973, with the poet hardly into his twenties. It is easy now perhaps, with the sheer size and continuity of his work, to take aspects of Muldoon for granted, but consider this from 'The Electric Orchard', published in that first collection:

> The belt would burst, the call be made
>
> The ambulance arrive and carry the faller away
> To hospital with a scream.

There and then the electric people might invent the
railway
Just watching the lid lifted by the steam.
Or decide that all laws should be based on gravity,
Just thinking of the faller fallen.
Even then they were running out of things to do and
see.

What is and remains astounding in that is the free
imaginative association caught alive, so to speak, in
the iron cage of complex stanzaic form, as if
Elizabeth Bishop's 'Man-moth' had coalesced with
Philip Larkin's 'Whitsun Weddings'. Remembering
the relative maturity of both those poets at the time
of their respective poems, we are confronted here
with an instance of accelerated poetic assimilation
akin to the young Keats' co-opting of a model from
Dryden for his May Odes. Whether the genius
involved is, in the last analysis, that of Keats or a
more sardonic technical wizard, Lord Byron, is
another question. But the fact remains that a poet in
his early twenties had by the start of the Seventies
already set a gold standard of melded imagination
and technique not only for his own contemporaries
but for a whole succeeding generation as well.

So far, so good. There is, however, a fly in the
ointment. With hindsight, it can be glimpsed in
even so excellent an early poem as 'The Field
Hospital'. Here, one's admiration for the deploy-
ment of an American Civil War image to suggest,
obliquely, certain issues of involvement or non-
involvement in a crisis nearer to home, is tempered
with awe that so young a poet could already create
so finished and detached an object, could distance
himself so completely. A little later, in the even-
better 'Lunch with Pancho Villa', detachment
seems to win out even more decisively,

"When are you going to tell the truth?" . . .
What should I say to this callow youth
Who learned to write last winter –
One of those correspondence courses –
And who's coming to lunch today?
he'll be rambling on, no doubt,
About pigs and trees, stars and horses.

These are superb poems, which validate that free-
floating realm of imagination outside of, if not necessarily opposed to, the brute facts of human suffering.
But they also introduce an emotional chill-factor
which culminates, ten years later, in the freeze-frames
of 'The More a Man Has, the More a Man Wants':

Once they collect his smithereens
he doesn't quite add up.
They're shy of a foot, and a calf
which stems
from his left shoe like a severely
pruned-back shrub.

Feeling has been too completely mastered. The
result, instead of poetic detachment, is something
approaching cynicism, a cornucopia of soapbox
violence, Americana and canned laughter. *But that's
the whole point*, the converted will chorus. *The
inability to feel anymore.* Unfortunately, the amoral
or the affectless are not their own best witness, and
we are back again with Keats and Byron, this time
from the angle of the heartfelt, and Keats' decrying
of Byron's "flash" poem, which "treats light things
seriously, and serious things lightly".

The Bret Easton Ellis side of Muldoon can also be
seen, though, as a kind of emotional defence-mecha-
nism which has picked itself apart gradually over the
years, towards the warmer, more intimately human
tones of the recent 'Incantata'. In that poem, despite
certain unevennessess, there is a mellowing with no
loss of power. Directly expressed emotion has never
come easily to this poet, and when it emerges through
the thickets of self-protective cleverness, it can sound
perilously close to sentimentality –

The fact that you were determined to cut yourself off
in your prime
because it was pre-determined has my eyes abrim:
('Incantata')

I try to imagine the strain
You must have been under, pretending to be right as
rain . . .
('Incantata')

– though it should be said that the uncertain
handling of personal emotion – it is there in 'The
Birth' and 'Bran' among others – is magnificently
overcome in the final lines of 'Incantata', one of the
highest points in Muldoon's work, and one of the
most moving expressions anywhere of art and
friendship in the shadow of non-existence:

than that the Irish Hermes,
Lugh, might have leafed through his vast herbarium
for the leaf that had it within it, Mary, to anoint and
anneal,

than that Lugh of the Long Arm might have found
in the midst of lus

na leac or lus na treatha or Frannc-lus,
in the midst of eyebright, or speedwell, or tansy, an
                                                   antidote,
than that this Incantata
might have you look up from your plate of copper or
                                                   zinc
on which you've etched the row upon row
of army-worms, than that you might reach out, arrah,
and take in your ink-stained hands my own hands
                                        stained with ink.

But all this is to jump ahead of the plot. As Kendall outlines it, there are the years of the Seventies and early Eighties working for the BBC in Belfast, whose corporate "back-stab / and leap-frog" is the background to his lament for Michael Heffernan in 'The Soap-Pig'. In the middle Eighties, after the association with Mary Powers detailed in 'Incantata', there is a second marriage and a move to America, where he now lives in Princeton, the objective correlatives for which are, loosely speaking, '7 Middagh Street' and 'Madoc'. Although these long poems from 'The Soap-Pig' onwards are many other things as well – explorations of love, friendship, philosophy and political commitment – it is hard not to see them as pretexts for autobiography, blueprints for an unwritten life story. And this suggests a possible explanation for the sheer size and extent of his poetic work so far – namely, his lack of a prose side. Bar a few minor pieces, he seems to have done without that other dimension most poets cultivate, to smite their enemies, outline their artistic credos or settle accounts with their past, whether personal or political. The midlife novel or autobiography, the book of critical essays, the regular reviewing spot. Instead, there has been an attempt to state everything in

purely mythopoeic terms, to be inclusive to the point of overstraining the forms themselves. Techniques and personae, be they fictional, cinematic or both, are sieved through forms that are essentially lyrical, with results that are sometimes weird rather than wonderful, as if two contending impulses, memory and imagination, were at war in the same text.

There are signs, though, that Muldoon's love affair with the long poem may be on the wane, if his disparaging remarks about that form in a recent American interview are to be believed. Sonnets, however, are unlikely to be shown the door, and even in an age which has rediscovered them with a vengeance, Muldoon's, from the obese to the anorexic, must set some kind of record for plasticity. It is a form he has over-used, and there is a sense, especially in the Gallery texts mentioned below, that it comes far too easily to him now. Nonetheless, some of his finest poems over the years have been in this form, such as 'Lull', 'Quoof', 'The Right Arm', or 'The Merman'.

He was ploughing his single
                           furrow
through the green, heavy
                           sward
Of water. I was sowing
                   winter wheat
At the shoreline, when our
                        farms met.

Not a furrow, quite, I argued.
Nothing would come of his
                        long acre
But breaker growing out of
                           breaker,
The wind-scythe, the rain-
                          harrow.

This, one of his most beautiful lyrics, comes from his second book *Mules* (1977). Along with others included here, such as 'Blemish', 'Our Lady of Ardboe', 'Armageddon' and the title poem, as well as some not included, this constitutes a small but real golden age in

Muldoon's work, a lost time temporarily obscured by the flashier stuff that has come since, when the poet stood in wonderment before the world, rather than hallucinating it, however brilliantly, in psilocybin dayglo, or shuffling it like a pack of culturally-marked cards. With 'Immram', from his next collection, we enter the Duty Free Zone of postmodern imagination he has wandered in ever since, where Eskimos get high on their own urine, cokesniffing women scrawl Helter Skelter on walls in their own blood, and surfboards are worshipped by the bare-assed. Only with recent poems like 'Cows' or 'Milkweed and Monarch' is there a sense of coming full circle again, of a middle-aged man rattling, however tentatively, the closed gates of his own Irish Eden.

In between the Faber volumes, there has been a longstanding association with Gallery Press in Ireland, beginning with *Immram* in 1980, running through *The Wishbone* (1984) to *The Prince of The Quotidian* (1994) and most recently *Kerry Slides* (1996). *Immram* and the lion's share of *The Wishbone* find their way into the new Faber selection. *Prince of the Quotidian*, apart from its one real poem 'The Sonogram', is sumptuously-produced domestic moodiness, published, if we are to believe Tim Kendall, against the poet's own better judgement. *Kerry Slides* is easier to like, and never less than technically adept. But it is very much the poet on holiday keeping his hand in, and there is little real pressure behind the work. A series of haiku-like glimpses, occasionally elegaic but mostly humorous, are book-ended by a sonnet of arrival and one of departure. The orneryness of Ireland comes through, but also (perhaps more so in the accompanying photographs) something of its chthonic force, and one senses, beneath the middle-class overlay, the undertow of loss in the valedictory poem,

> Our last night in Dingle we eat in "Doyle's"
> where the redoubtable John and Stella
> serve scallops tossed in "extra virgin" oil
> in honour of James of Compostella,
>
> the patron saint of Dingle and the stay
> of pilgrims and those peripatetics

who have, like us, "shook off their gowns of clay" to ponder the Eudemian Ethics.

Kerry Slides, though a minor variant on the larger circlings of departure and return, is nothing new in itself, while *Six Honest Serving Men* (1995) another in the Gallery series and the text of a short play produced in Princeton, is, if anything, a regression to the emotionally-anaesthetised world of 'The More A Man Has . . .' where remarkably articulate IRA men engage in rhymed wordplay while violence happens offstage. This it is impossible to judge without seeing, but it does enough to suggest that the warmth and mellowness of 'Incantata', placed though it is at the end of *New Selected Poems*, may not be the new start or happy ending many would like it to be.

An interesting paradox with Muldoon is how, in spite of his apparent weirdness, he has always been acceptable to a collegiate middle-class world that dotes on him more and more the stranger his work becomes, and that seems to be ageing gracefully with him now. With the arrival of Tim Kendall's full-length study, the process of absorption seems complete. Jonah — still alive, one hopes — takes his ease in the belly of the academic whale, watching a little guardedly from the cover of this "first book on Muldoon". It is what one might expect — excellent biographical and textual background, acres of cross-referencing and information-retrieval, not a spark of intuition. Kendall is the tortoise to Muldoon's hare, and the results, depressing or hilarious depending on your viewpoint, will be welcomed by students wanting someone else to do their reading for them, or used as ammunition by those for whom this poet's success is owed to his providing exegetical fodder for academics with careers to build. It seems to me a valuable book, and its even-handed gaze brings into focus neglected texts like *Shining Brow*, a couple of punchy extracts from which are included in the *New Selected*:

> Nineteen twelve. The Greeks and Turks
> fight a familiar duel.
> The Piltdown Men of Planter Stock

Up went the Trump Towers and Canary Wharfs of the imagination ... Inside, in desacralised space, a brilliant trader in mythic stocks and shares was breaking the bank, while down in the basement, unheard, a Howard-Hughesian double muttered "I'd love to write beautifully pellucid simple lyric poems"

scuttle Irish Home Rule.
The Titanic founders on a berg.
The passengers cry wee-wee-wee.
Going down,
Going down,
Going down in history.

Words like "technique" and "technical" abound, and Kendall can seem like a man rapt at state-of-the-art plumbing and wiring who never questions the soullessness of the building as a whole. Unsurprisingly, he prefers poems like 'The More A Man Has ...' or 'Yarrow', where he can set to work on a complex of allusions or be dazzled by "intercut" and "exploded" sestinas, as if these of themselves constituted poetic authenticity. Praise is almost always technical praise, but it is left to others – Sean Dunne, for instance, or John Carey – to ask the awkward questions, while Kendall withdraws into neutral silence at crucial moments. Faced with this useful but over-cautious book, let me stick my own neck out then, with "a moral, a moral for our times".

Muldoon, a great user of myths, was himself used by the myth of the Eighties. His Seventies work, some of which seems to me his finest, flowed underground from *Why Brownlee Left* in a trickle of lyrics, mainly about his father. Recently, it has tried to resurface here and there, through the swallow-holes of individual lyrics, or the lacustrine 'Incantata'. Meanwhile 'Immram' (1980) arrived bang on time for the boom years. Up went the Trump Towers and Canary Wharfs of the imagination, dazzling in their gigantism. Inside, in desacralised space, a brilliant trader in mythic stocks and shares was breaking the bank, while down in the basement, unheard, a Howard-Hughesian double muttered "I'd love to write beautifully pellucid simple lyric poems". Along came the Nineties, our stockbroker retired, and mows his lawn clevercleverclever in Princeton. Six hours to the east, at moonrise over Keenaghan and Collegelands, a doppelganger sits at a lit window, in the benign shadow of his mother. Amazingly young for his age, he is writing *Muldoon: The Hidden Years*, his new collection. It will consist of beautifully pellucid simple lyric poems.

Harry Clifton's latest collection is *Night Train Through the Brenner*.

Homing Pigeon

by Dennis O'Driscoll

MIROSLAV HOLUB
Supposed to Fly
translated by Ewald Osers,
Bloodaxe, £8.95,
ISBN 1 85224 274 4

NOBODY WHO IS familiar with Miroslav Holub's original and experimental output would expect him to publish an orthodox autobiography. Indeed, nobody who is aware of Holub's lifelong determination to produce hard-centred rather than self-centred work would expect an autobiography from him in the first place. Steeped since childhood in the ancient classics, he relishes the fact that Homer, the greatest of all poets, casts "no biographical shadow" and, "in his blindness", neglected to behave sensationally enough to have acquired a marketable "personality".

Holub, who would doubtless be happy to share Homer's anonymity, once said: "When you give a scientific lecture or make a scientific paper, there is no personal background given: no age, no numbers of girlfriends or wives or children. Nothing. So why should these be analysed in poetry?" *Supposed to Fly*, a book of reminiscences – arranged as a "suite" of poems, short prose pieces and photographs – keeps us in the dark about numbers of wives and children, although we do catch sight of the incipient scientist engaged in "late-evening experiments" with his girlfriend. If *Supposed to Fly* is a family album, it is one full of double and triple exposures as Holub's thoughts veer entrancingly off in all directions. To be accurate, this is less a collection of reminiscences than a book prompted by personal experiences, the poetry and prose dipped in a bright solution of irony and imagery.

The centre of gravity – not to mention levity – of *Supposed to Fly* is Holub's birthplace, Plzeň (or Pilsen), a city famous for beer and Skodas (and, presumably, drunken drivers also). Holub's name means "pigeon" and in this book – published in Czech in 1994, to mark the 700th anniversary of his native city – he becomes something of a homing pigeon. It was a swift rather than a pigeon which gobbled the fly at the end of Holub's most famous poem; and there is more than a dash of Jonathan Swift in Holub's pungent wit and his frequent adjustments of scale (the latter additionally influenced by a lifetime of gazing down microscopes).

Holub gets his facts straight by telling oblique truths, by letting all kinds of parallels meet, as they do "when we draw them by our own hand". Yet, far from confessional though the reminiscences may be, they reveal more of the private Holub than any of his previous books: riding his scooter to meet his father coming from the office, winning a photograph of a local hero in a "football chocolate competition", enduring Sunday outings with his parents on "privilege" train tickets (his father worked for the railways). Having so often in his poems provided a child's-eye view of the adult world, he proves himself equally skilled at an adult depiction of his childhood world.

Intellectually outstanding though he clearly is, Holub never flaunts his mental riches any more than he blinds us with science. Admittedly, he slips in the odd scientific word or phrase ("paradichlorbenzene", "oxidative phosphorylisation"), but he does so in the same spirit in which a poet might invoke an obscure but expressive placename. It is his ready access to so many disparate areas of knowledge, and the playful intelligence and limber imagination to link them, which accounts for his improvised and ingenious use of multi-stranded metaphors: Pilseners are "neutral as annelid worms in the land of Canaan"; rosaries have "threaded pearl-like / molecules of antibodies to words"; a summer-house is "the personal germ of the Tower of Babel, cut short in its evolution like the coccyx".

Another of Holub's characteristics is his Audenesque ability to find satisfyingly epigrammatic formulas for things, defining and illuminating in one deft stroke. Spontaneous aphorisms, like the springs in Auden's limestone, "spurt out everywhere with a chuckle" – in the prose, poetry and even in the captions he provides for the highly dispensable black-and-white photographs which mingle with this least monochrome of texts: "The essence of art is / that we're not much good at it"; "every park is by definition infinite and mythical"; "stupidity multiplies in a herd, whereas reason is divided by the number of heads, and reason thus diminishes with multitude".

Supposed to Fly reprints some of Holub's early work, including 'Five Minutes after the Air Raid', 'A Dog in the Quarry' and 'How to Paint a Perfect Christmas', poems which have long entered the bloodstream of English-language readers. There are many new poems also; and, if not always as impressive as the meandering, mesmerising prose (which includes fascinating accounts of wartime Pilsen), they nonetheless mark a return to his best form. On the whole, this volume is his most satisfying since the Penguin *Selected Poems* of 1967, a year when Holub recalls returning home from America to "darkness as when a whale swallows not only the sun and the moon but also the enlightenment".

Towards the end of the book, he muses that, had the 700th anniversary of Pilsen occurred a few years earlier, it would have been celebrated with the "installation of a red star on the tower of St Bartholomew's church" and "decorations for several Red Army men who had served incognito in the US army". But, thanks to superlative timing, the city instead underwent a five-star face-lift and it was Holub himself who was decorated, receiving a silver medal as a "Meritorious Native of Pilsen". With the publication of *Supposed to Fly*, a gold medal is surely called for.

Dennis O'Driscoll's latest collections are *Long Story Short* (Anvil) and *The Bottom Line* (Dedalus).

Poetry with an Airbag

by David Kennedy

Emergency Kit: poems for strange times

eds. Jo Shapcott & Matthew Sweeney,
Faber, £9.99,
ISBN 0 571 17207 5

WHEN PETER FORBES asked me to review this book, I was acutely aware of being handed a predetermined cultural role – co-editor of last anthology pronounces on new anthology – so I want to start by dissociating myself entirely from the small scale media construction that has been called "the anthology wars". In fact, I've always been a conscientious objector but because of this predetermined role, my responsibilities as a critic need restating: to locate not only the quality of the work under review but its identity and position as a cultural product. As Susan Rubin Sulieman points out in her invigorating book *Risking Who One Is*, although contemporary works are "less 'safe' to write about than works of the past [because they] bring the critic's self into play, into risk", the risk should be embraced "for the sake of self-recognition, an expanded historical awareness, and a sense of at least potential collective action". Since compiling an anthology is an act of criticism, I think this applies to editors too. Criticising the contemporary, Sulieman argues, allows us to discover a sense of "intersection" with other people and their lives, the sense that

> for a number of years we breathed the same air and
> participated in at least some aspects of the same
> material culture (for example, knowing what a tele
> phone is, or an airplane, or a radio, even if you have
> never used one).

Sulieman's concept of "intersection" goes right to the heart of *Emergency Kit*, whose subtitle and introduction attempt very self-consciously to place both the book itself and poetry at the end of the century in a shared material culture. Shapcott and Sweeney have collected over 220 poems in English from around the world, stretching from the mid-1950s to the present, in order to compile "the anthology we wish we could have read when we were starting out". They identify a poetry "which

fulfils Robert Frost's demand that it should be 'a fresh look and a fresh listen'"; a poetry "whose distorting vision breaks through to the truth"; and a poetry which shows the art "can be fun and a serious matter at the same time". The poets chosen include: Eiléan Ní Chuilleanáin, Arun Kolatkar, Tanure Ojaide, Odia Ofeimun, Elizabeth Spires, Imtiaz Dharker, A. K. Ramanujan, Kojo Gyinye Kyei, Belle Waring, George Awoonor-Williams and everyone else from Auden to Judith Wright. If a starting point in the mid-1950s suggests that history is, so to speak, getting shorter then it's worth noting part of the answer Shapcott and Sweeney give to their own question "But why the need for such poetry now?":

> It occurs to us that, just as Donne and Marvell were
> compelled by the discoveries of their time, the early
> seventeenth century, so the poets in this book are
> responding to or reflecting the surprises of ours.
> TV, tabloids, movies, virtual reality, the Internet –
> all these have encouraged us to take the extraordi
> nary for granted. We have watched men walk on the
> moon, we talk to each other across space and time,
> we conduct our business and our courtships on the
> 'net'. Isn't it inevitable, then, that these days poetry
> should be written which makes free with the bound
> aries of realism, crossing this way and that, at will?

What *Emergency Kit*'s introduction describes, then, is not self-recognition or historical awareness but self-consciousness and this is where both introduction and anthology, perhaps unintentionally, do capture something important.

Our culture commodifies and sells back to us what we exclude and feel threatened by and, because we can't decide if this is sophisticated or decadent, we get the sense of "mingledness" that is fundamental to the way we live now and makes our millennial culture so listless. This is caught perfectly by Maurice Riordan's 'Time Out' which imagines how quickly the urban idyll can become a nightmare but then safely withdraws into the predominant systems of exchange and value: "Let us get *this* dad in and out of the shop, safely across the street, / Safely indoors again, less a couple of quid, plus the listings mags / And ten Silk Cut, back on board the sofa: reprieved, released, relaxed".

The interweaving of assimilation and exclusion has wider ramifications. Anthologies mark the point at which the excluded is assimilated, at which opposition becomes establishment. This was the case with *MoMo* and *The New Poetry*. *Emergency Kit* wants to mark the point at which contemporary poetry becomes "easy" and popular, hence the editors' reassertion of "realism" as the benchmark. This reassertion is characteristically British as is the feeling that realism *per se* is not quite good enough. Here, the introduction assimilates the excluded in a different way. Shapcott and Sweeney tell us that although they "made an early decision to limit our attention to poems written in English", *Emergency Kit* "shares an imaginative landscape" with poetry that was

> often written under oppression, its oblique, riddling and parable-like procedures allowing it to say things the censor couldn't pick up. The effect of the best of this writing had been so direct and profound [...] that many English-language poets of the period under consideration have either consciously or unconsciously absorbed it.

Apart from confirming a widely held suspicion that half of contemporary poetry is written by the barely conscious, this gives an impoverished model of significant experience and the value of reading writers outside one's home culture. Most importantly, it describes how the poetry of Western democracies can add street cred to its habitual language of gender and objects and the predominant model of poetry as self-absorbed, dissident individualism.

The reason for invoking and excluding poets like Holub is that they remind us that poetry is difficult: not in the sense of being obscure, élitist or lexically arcane but in the way their poetry enacts a *thinking through* of difficulty. This absence perhaps explains why *Emergency Kit* is so reminiscent of old school anthologies like *Voices*. Like *Emergency Kit*, such anthologies did show that poetry could be "fun and a serious matter" but they also made everything look alike, equally consumable. In its pursuit of populism, *Emergency Kit* not only homogenises but misrepresents as well – it even manages to make John Ashbery look cosily allegorical! And like *Voices*, poets and poetry are removed from their cultural contexts so that Allen Ginsberg is washed clean of any inconvenient political and sexual radicalism and Allen Curnow is divorced from his crucial identity as a spiritual pilgrim in the postmodern age. The challenges and rewards of their work come as much from context as inherent virtues or, to put it another way, put Peter Didsbury in New York and he looks ordinary. Part of the

problem I have with *Emergency Kit* is that so many of its 200 plus poems are either bad or boring. Instead of getting a large anthology of poems which play off each other in surprising ways what actually results is a continuum of "fun" or dully descriptive poetry in which really good work inevitably suffers by association. If you really wanted to compile an anthology that demonstrated Shapcott's and Sweeney's claims you'd start with Paul Muldoon – not George Mackay Brown! Consequently, *Emergency Kit* actually manages to suggest that all the "talking up" of contemporary poetry over the last four years or so has, in fact, been a massive failure of consciousness.

So is *Emergency Kit* a return to the gentility principle? Not quite but it is, I think, clearly part of the post-NGP, media-friendly New Populism. I just wish the New Populism wasn't veering ever closer to saying "Oh dear, there aren't enough people visiting the National Gallery so we'd better have an exhibition of Pamela Anderson posters". If I was a cynic, I'd say that Faber are trying to cash in. My proof copy misprints "ocarina" – a small musical instrument – as "acarina" which is a machine designed by publishers for making a lot of money. If I believed that culture is more than random responses to economic imperatives, I'd say that British poetry was revolted by the mirror *The New Poetry* held up to its self-congratulatory posturings about politicisation and greater all round inclusiveness and the result is New Populism and *Emergency Kit*. But *Emergency Kit* is also as much of our times as New Labour, so we shouldn't be too beastly to the messengers. And maybe it has been compiled with an eye on the classroom – school and creative writing – but, if so, let's not pretend it's anything to do with "strange times". I don't mean I wanted more poems about AIDS or East Timor but I would have appreciated, particularly from Jo Shapcott who has written 'Phrasebook', one of the key English poems of the late twentieth century, a stronger sense of just how "strange" the times are and how poetry can respond. Example: The Industrial Revolution created great poverty *and* improved economic opportunity. The late twentieth century has seen Western countries creating an underclass in times of zero economic growth. Strange? We just don't have a clue, do we?

David Kennedy's critical book, *New Relations* (Seren) is reviewed on p. 5.

Light my Fire

by Jamie McKendrick

OCTAVIO PAZ
The Double Flame:
Essays on Love and Eroticism

translated by Helen Lane,
Harvill, £14.99,
ISBN 1 86046 250 2

IN THIS BOOK of essays Octavio Paz argues that the way love as a subject has been marginalised by our society is evidence not only of apostasy to the great cultural tradition which grew out of Provençal poetry but also of a progressive devaluation of what he calls the "human person". He shows himself to be a wonderfully erudite guide through the history of discourses on love from Plato's *Symposium* by way, among many others, of Tibullus and Propertius, Dante, Quevedo to Breton, with reference to philosophy as well as contemporary science. The reader is likely to suffer a certain amount of travel fatigue from this briskly knowledgeable survey, and many of the stopping places are well-trodden. His reference to Dante for example deals conveniently with the Paolo and Francesca episode. He concedes that many scholars have written all kinds of interesting things about it but for him the most important point is that Dante fainted in response to Francesca's tale. This leaves us with a non-too-enquiring Romantic vision of Dante, a position that suits Paz who is writing to extol the humanistic panacea of love. His enlistment of Dante in this cause involves a certain amount of legerdemain. Paolo and Francesca have been placed in hell, and it is likely that Dante is advancing, through Francesca's dazzling but flawed rhetoric, a critique of the courtly love tradition as well as of his own passionate susceptibility to it.

What Paz is offering in these essays is essentially a creed and a last testament: "Love does not defeat death; it is a wager against time and its accidents. Through love we catch a glimpse, in this life, of the other life. Not of eternal life, but as I have tried to say in several poems, of pure vitality". Yet for all the culture dauntingly within his reach the writing is strangely remote from the existential upheaval and renewal and risk that are involved in the experience of love. Though only taking two months to write in a state of "joyous desperation", the book, the introduction tells us, had been planned, begun, abandoned, restarted over a period of many years. I suspect that whilst its cultural freight may have been lighter had it been written closer to the experience which prompted it in India in 1965, the writing would have been more vivid and intriguing.

For a book of this type generalisations are unavoidable, but Paz generalises in a serenely confident manner, and often his claims can seem merely bizarre. For example, in the early part of the book, he writes that "violence is a necessary component of sexuality". How necessary and necessary to whom? This remark may be glossed by a passage in his *Labyrinth of Solitude* (1961) where, speaking of the Mexican expression "*hijo de la Chingada*" he explains "in effect every woman – even if she gives herself willingly to the man – is torn open, is *la Chingada*". Yet the vision of sexuality it reveals is reductive and unconvincing.

Another example is when he speaks of the friendship of women: "in relationships between women, backbiting, envy, gossip and petty perfidies are frequent. Which is almost certainly owing not to any innate inability of women but to their social situation. Perhaps their progressive liberation will change all this. I hope so". Something to look forward to. It probably hasn't crossed Paz's mind that this sentence could be read as anything but evidence of his enlightened benevolence. Paz has actually made a career out of writing like this – as in this passage from *Labyrinth of Solitude*: "Woman is another figure who lives apart and is therefore an enigmatic figure. It would be better to say that she is the Enigma. She attracts and repels like men of an alien race or nationality. She is an image of fecundity and death …". This kind of prose writes itself, and must have a reward in the heaven of pseudo-philosophy as well as on earth – judging by the honours that have been showered on Paz's work from the Premio Cervantes to the Nobel Prize.

Rafael Doniz

Grudging Lyrical Earth

By Anne Stevenson

GEORGE SZIRTES
Selected Poems
Oxford Poets, £9.99,
ISBN 0 19 283223 9

THE FORCE AND ORIGINALITY of George Szirtes' poems can be traced to his Jewish origins in Hitler's and then Stalin's Transylvania, to his initiation as an artist in England, and to his liking for American poets of refined technique such as John Crowe Ransom and Anthony Hecht: an unusual cocktail, but in Szirtes' case productive of a tone and style unlike anyone else's. His poems are impossible to "place". Open the book at random. If your eyes fall on lines like "The Man who is a Cello and the Fish who plays / The Violin are suddenly struck dumb. / The Goat in the Sky grows horns of logic", you may think you've struck a vein of mid-European surrealism. And yes, 'The Green Mare's Advice to the Cows' is a homage to Marc Chagall and the colourful irony of Chagall's politics. Flick back the pages, say, to 'Porch', and you stand with George Herbert in the antichamber of love, religious and secular, "not daring / to approach the altar" in an "interregnum" between "the kissing place" and a great god's consummated passion. Herbert is invoked by name, and then again by the way these metaphysical verses confine their meaning to metaphor.

A number of remarkable poems, particularly three long, ambitious ones that draw on events of Szirtes' Hungarian past, take place in a sort of meditative eternity. Szirtes' way with time is to treat it as a continuous, diaphanous illusion. Thus in 'The Photographer in Winter' the poet's young mother (who was indeed a photographer) controls from behind the lens of her camera the photographic stills of a future from which her son simultaneously photographs her.

Camera angles, convincing details. Please
Co-operate with me, and turn your head,
Smile vacantly as if you were not dead
But walked through parallel worlds. Now look at me
As though you really meant it. I think we could be
Good for each other. Hold it right there. Freeze.

The organisation of this eight-page exploration of memory and love – four six-line stanzas per page, the first and last lines sealing their rhyme around two sets of couplets – prevents nostalgia from ever getting an upper hand.

A looser, more difficult stanza-pattern regulates Szirtes' meditation on buried, still-echoing resonances in 'Metro', which must be reckoned a major contribution to post-war European literature. Read it carefully and see why! Using a painter-like collage of images to retrieve lost times, lives, cities and betrayed hopes, Szirtes weaves his personal and historical themes into this work of profound psychological complexity. Yet the material of his memory is always exact.

The smell of old women now creeps over me,
An insect friction against bone
And spittle, and an ironed dress
Smoother than shells gathered by the sea,
A tongue between her teeth like a scrap
Of cloth, and an eye of misted glass . . .

'Metro' can be read as an elaborate allegory of the unconscious, with its undertone of collective desire (it takes as its epigraph Derek Mahon's line "What should they do there but desire?"), but what is most impressive is that the poem and its form are indissoluble. Writing it, Szirtes must have allowed his theme to establish a thirteen-line stanza which, with its loose iambic rhythm and pattern of end-rhymes, turned out to be sturdy enough to steer inchoate emotions into coherent images, and therefore into poetic effectiveness. The same could be said for nearly every one of these *Selected Poems*. A few mannerisms may mar one or two early experiments, but by the time Szirtes was writing 'The Swimmers' and 'The Buttonmaker's Tale' he was a master. 'Transylvana' is nearly as remarkable as 'Metro' for its welding of theme and form – in *terza rima* this time. The entire volume is as well shaped as each individual poem, beginning with the poet's learning English in the process of coming to terms with human sorrow in a strange world, and ending with the tantalisingly ambiguous 'Soil' that roots the aspiring artist in a "grudging lyrical earth" where he's caught like a violin

scraped and scratched, and there is nowhere to go
but home, which is nowhere to be found
and yet
is here, unlost, solid, the very ground
on which you stand; but cannot visit
or know.

THE CLASSIC POEM

SELECTED BY E. A. MARKHAM

AS THE REQUEST is for a 'classic' not a 'best' poem, this isn't a strenuous exercise. A choice of Kamau Brathwaite's cameo turns would have included 'Rites' (the most compelling bit of cricket commentary I know – the prose version is good, too!); 'The Dust' (Barbados women at their idiomatic, funny, philosophical best); 'Stone' (the dirge for Jamaican poet, Michael Smith – painful & celebratory) or just something with a fun name ('Ouagadougou') etc. 'Wings of a Dove' is from the book-length *Rights of Passage* (1967), the first part of a trilogy tracking Africans in the diaspora, then in Africa (*Masks*), finally to the Caribbean (*Islands*) – brought together in one volume, *The Arrivants* (1973). *Rights of Passage*, read by the author at the Jeanetta Cochrane Theatre in 1967 (at the first Caribbean Artists' Movement conference), is classic in its shock of impact, in the Walcott vs. Brathwaite debate it stimulated – particularly 'Wings' which is also representative of early Brathwaite. (Kamau, like Walcott, was born in 1930.)

What is classic Brathwaite? Outrageous puns, word-salads more tasty than Lucky's in *Godot*, modernist switching of linguistic registers, language stained equally by Revelation and by rastaspeak, delight in rhetoric – from a griot, a shaman, holy fool missing pulpit and court. What else? An obsession with African jazz-folk, nation language. Enough of that is reflected in 'Wings'.

It's useful to know that Brathwaite speaks (and sings) his poems well (Barbados & Cambridge, and songs learnt in Ghana), so that this act of reclamation, even at its more-intellectually robust is not 'academic'. (Let's say he's as playful, easily, as Zukofsky, and less puzzling than the performances of Lenny Henry or Trevor McDonald.) Brathwaite's schema – over 19 books of poetry, plus recordings, essays, poemstories etc. – can be faulted: too easy appropriation of the mother image (Africa, Barbados, Lake Chad) or a weakness for what the poet Mimi Khalvati, in another context, calls 'global' (larger than local) colour. But Brathwaite is a resource as well as a poet. Some have benefited directly (Linton Kwesi Johnson), the rest of us, by being made more literate about history, indirectly.

E. A. Markham's latest book, *Misapprehensions* (Anvil), was reviewed in *PR* Vol 85 No 4.

KAMAU BRATHWAITE
WINGS OF A DOVE

1.

Brother Man the Rasta
man, beard full of lichens
brain full of lice
watched the mice
come up through the floor-
boards of his down-
town, shanty-town kitchen,
and smiled. Blessed are the poor
in health, he mumbled,
that they should inherit this
wealth. Blessed are the meek
hearted, he grumbled,
for theirs is this stealth.

Brother Man the Rasta
man, hair full of lichens
head hot as ice
watched the mice
walk into his poor
hole, reached for his peace
and the pipe of his ganja
and smiled how the mice
eyes, hot pumice
pieces, glowed into his room
like ruby, like rhinestone
and suddenly startled like
diamond.

And I
Rastafar-I
in Babylon's boom
town, crazed by the moon
and the peace of this chalice, I
prophet and singer, scourge
of the gutter, guardian
Trench Town, the Dungle and Young's
Town, rise and walk through the now silent
streets of affliction, hawk's eyes
hard with fear, with
affection, and hear my people
cry, my people
shout:

Down down
white
man, con
man, brown
man, down
down full
man, frown-
ing fat
man, that
white black
man that
lives in
the town.

Rise rise
locks-
man, Solo-
man wise
man, rise
rise rise
leh we
laugh
dem, mock
dem, stop
dem, kill
dem an' go
back back
to the black

man lan'
back back
to Af-
rica.

2.

Them doan mean it, yuh know,
them cahn help it
but them clean-face browns in
Babylon town is who I most fear

an' who fears most I.
Watch de vulture dem a-fly-
in', hear de crow a-dem crow
see what them money a-buy?

Caw caw caw caw.
Ol' crow, ol' crow, cruel ol'
ol' crow, that's all them got
to show.

Crow fly flip flop
hip hop
pun de ground; na
feet feel firm

pun de firm stones; na
good pickney born
from de flesh
o' dem bones;

naw naw naw naw.

3.

So beat dem drums
dem, spread

dem wings dem,
watch dem fly

dem, soar dem
high dem,
clear in the glory of the Lord.

Watch dem ship dem
come to town dem

full o' silk dem
full o' food dem

an' dem 'plane dem
come to groun' dem

full o' flash dem
full o' cash dem

silk dem food dem
shoe dem wine dem

that dem drink dem
an' consume dem

praisin' the glory of the Lord.

So beat dem burn
dem, learn

dem that dem
got dem nothin'

but dem
bright bright baubles

that will burst dem
when the flame dem

from on high dem
raze an' roar dem

an' de poor dem
rise an' rage dem

in de glory of the Lord.

Caught on a Train

by Ian McMillan

NEIL ROLLINSON
A Spillage of Mercury
Cape Poetry, £7.00,
ISBN 0 224 04008 1

ROBERT REHDER
The Compromises Will be Different
Carcanet, £8.95,
ISBN 1 85754 127 8

IAN POPLE
The Glass Enclosure
Arc, £5.95,
ISBN 1 900072 00 9

ELEANOR BROWN
Maiden Speech
Bloodaxe, £6.95,
ISBN 1 85224 351 1

MICHAEL GLOVER
Impossible Horizons
Sinclair Stevenson, £7.99,
ISBN 1 85619 612 7

I TEND TO DO a lot of my reading and writing on trains, scribbling away as the train judders and halts, zooms and stops. I've had a lot of train journeys recently, and these first collections have been splendid travelling companions.

Neil Rollinson

I tackled Neil Rollinson between Sheffield and Bristol Temple Meads, and he was a delight as the sun came up over Chesterfield; from the first poem it's obvious that we're in the company of a fresh and original writer, creating off-kilter stories of Modern Life, peering with a truly fresh eye at the tried-and-tested. Here's the opening of his poem 'A List of Requirements for the end of the World': "A barrel of beer, two glasses, / a coal fire, toasting forks / and muffins, a little bacon, sausages. / Near the fire, a bed, a double bed / with cool white sheets, preferably silk". It's a poem created The Rollinson Way: a gentle building up of detail, a sharp ear for

rhythm, a clear eye for the absurd; later in the poem, the requirements include "A broken television / stuck in the corner. A radio jammed / on Hilversum". Rollinson continually surprised me, as the train rolled through Derby and Burton-on-Trent. There's a poem called 'Giant Puffballs' that begins "Can I make it home, or do I shit / in the woods?", and ends with a beautiful meditation on the puffballs: "Pregnant as fish bowls, weird as a hedgeful / of skulls. I pull one out of its hole / gentle as a midwife, palping the domed head in my hands".

Rollinson writes very well about sex, and indeed the opening lines of 'Cornucopia' had me more or less tumescent as we passed through Cheltenham, which is quite a frightening thought: "It lies on his thing, dribbling, / dead to the world. She kisses him / she's not finished yet; she squeezes / the limp flesh like a pastry cook / between her fingers. He groans. / He's had enough. She takes the slob / of it into her mouth / and tickles the head". If Rollinson can keep the promise of this first book, then he'll be travelling first class before too long.

Robert Rehder

rode with me on the slow, beautiful line between Barnsley and Huddersfield, which is sort-of appropriate, not just because many of his lines are slow and beautiful, but because there's a lot of that indefinable quality called Huddersfield in his poems. He's an American writer who is now Professor of English and American Literature at Fribourg in the Suisse Romande, and the poems are wonderfully chatty snapshots and philosophical tracts about, if you'll pardon the repetition, Modern Life. You feel that you're drawn into his world; it's as though you're reading a diary, or letters, or the inside of someone's head: "I'm tired. / All I want to do is read, if that – / / I keep losing my place. / Even before I started painting the house" ('Sunset'). The poems are oddly inconsequential and of great consequence at the same time; take 'Corminboeuf 157' for instance, which opens delightfully: "I am writing these poems / As fast as I can / So that I do not miss out on my late style / which will be extremely allusive, / / Very simple, Freer than anything I've Ever done". Because of this playfulness, you get an enormous sense of possibility as you read these poems; a sense of what is possible in a poem, a sense that you get when you read writers as diverse as, say, Jackson Mac Low or Adrian

Mitchell (Oops! Dropped names on the line! Hope the train can get past them!). The poems, frail-looking and idiosyncratic as they are (each one in couplets, many of them with titles borrowed from *Moby Dick*) nevertheless take on the Big Concerns: History, Place, Language, Art. ("The weakness of painting / As a language is / That it's not used / for anything else".) This book had me grinning all over my face as we rolled into Huddersfield station, and there aren't many books you can say that about.

Ian Pople

It's astonishing how quickly you can get from Doncaster to London these days; one hour and twenty-five minutes is the fastest one, and I had a daytrip there to absorb Ian Pople's first full-length collection; I like Pople's work anyway, and as the world whizzed past my window I marvelled again at his ability to somehow pack each line with more detail than actually seems to be there at first glance in the few words. I know that all poetry should do this, but you know that it doesn't. This is the opening of 'Park View Road' from the sequence 'A Local Sense': "Light clung to umbrellas / in the studio. She wore / her hair up and a mohair jumper / / and I had my hand upon her shoulder. / In our mother's bungalow / that photo stands upon the wooden box / of cutlery my mother also gave". They say that if you're on a train and you look out of the window at an object in the middle distance like a tree, say, then the whole of the land-

Eleanor Brown

scape appears to revolve around that object, and that's what Ian Pople's poems are like; they seem to concentrate everything around them until they become the centre of whatever they are describing. I know that all poetry should do that, but you know that it doesn't.

As the train slowed towards London I wished my journey was longer so that I could savour more of Pople, try and figure out how he worked his magic, but as the train stopped at King's Cross I decided to leave it as magic; not good for a critic, maybe, but bliss for a reader: "Behind me the garden descends to water. / Each night a balloon drifts over the river, / gas jets strain the silence / and trout rise into the shadows" ('Basle').

Eleanor Brown

I read Eleanor Brown on a late-night train from Manchester back to Sheffield after my regular stint reading and talking about poems on Radio 1. The 00.16 is always quiet, and this particular midnight I was the only person on it, so I felt like it was just me and Eleanor on the whole train. After we went through Stockport, though, I felt like Wendy Cope and Sophie Hannah were in the carriage with us, because at first glance Eleanor Brown's work is very Copesque and Sophiesticated: "It's not that I think she is vapid and silly / It's not that her voice makes me wince / but chilli con carne without any chilli / is only a plateful of mince".

By the time we got to the Edale Tunnel, though, it was just me-an'-Eleanor, and the reason for that is the ambitious fully-realised sequence of fifty sonnets that's the centrepiece of the book. The sonnets chart a love affair, from tentative beginning ("Six minutes silence, as you first caressed / my hand, which was tacitly received, / first, physical, deliberate, overt, / licensed acknowledgement of your desire") through burning passion (when you lie sprawled across my sweat-soaked breast, / one arm outflung across the crumpled bed – / only a sated animal at rest; / only a boy whose mistress strokes his head;") to parting ("Come back to me, before some other voice / can come and drown some memory of mine / far off; come here, before some fresher tone / can overcome whatever tones mine had / that pleased you once") to a final more-than-acceptance ("…and still my dear / and still, I say you were a good idea".) After the watershed of the hefty sonnet sequence, the poems seem even less Wendy Copey, and as we got to Sheffield I knew that Eleanor Brown had, and would develop further, her own voice, as in 'Beauty and the Prince Formerly Known as Beast', when the Prince's lover remembers the beast behind the prince's soft touch: "Then I remember how he looked at me / under that curse, when I would go to bed, / deep-set eyes burning in his shaggy head / – he used to look at me quite hungrily. / / With this most gentle of all gentlemen, / it would be wrong to ask for that again; / / I don't. But on my own, some nights at least, / I lie and wish, a little, for my beast".

Michael Glover

There's a little one-carriage train that scuttles between Barnsley and Wakefield every hour; it only takes twenty minutes, and I knew it wouldn't be long enough to wrestle with Michael Glover's stout (140pp) collection. Still, it would be a start. Luckily (or unluckily, depending on whether you're reading poems on the train or not) we stopped for a long time just the other side of Darton, and I settled into the book as the other passengers tutted and fanned themselves with their tickets. I found myself wishing, after a while, that Michael Glover was sitting beside me, because I knew that he'd be able transform the drab, post industrial landscape outside into something thrilling. In a recent issue of *Verse*, Charles Simic wrote that the writing of a prose poem was "a bit like trying to catch a fly in a dark room. The fly probably isn't even there, the fly is inside your head, still, you keep tripping over and bumping into things while in hot pursuit".

Michael Glover doesn't write prose poems, but in its fly-in-a-dark-room way, Simic's description is an accurate encapsulation of the fuzziness and oddness of Glover's work. 'A Surrealist Lost in the Himalayas' for example, begins "These snow-driven summits have no hands. / They consist of nothing but / White, sleeveless tents. / No sooner do I pack / One blizzard away into a box / of such and such dimensions / Than it springs out again". The blurb refers to the "beguiling smell of France" in Glover's work, and there's certainly a lack of the plodding from A to B you sometimes find in English Poetry. The poems range from memories of childhood ("An outside lavvy's not a bad thing though, / Especially when the greens make you feel sick. / I stuffed them in my cheeks like hamsters do, / And shot them out in bits. The water flicked") to poems about poetry ("This is a poem factory. Do not enter. / The noxious stench of gases will clear / When the product emerges, / Colourless, pristine and definitive, / In the fullness of time future".) and poems that contain Philosophical Nuggets ("Each life has its own separate balcony / To which a man or woman ascends / From the fury of the office or the bedroom / To sip at the sweetness of air thinning down / From everywhere and nowhere, Yet never too soon".)

From Rollinson to Glover is a long journey, but it seems to me, as I buy yet another ticket for yet another journey, that poetry, unlike the railways, is safe in many different hands.

Hot Air

by Jonathan Davidson

MONIZA ALVI
A Bowl of Warm Air

Oxford Poets, £6.99,
ISBN 0 19 282520 8

W. N. HERBERT
Cabaret McGonagall

Bloodaxe, £7.95,
ISBN 1 85224 353 8

MONIZA ALVI WRITES a close and private poetry. In *A Bowl of Warm Air* we are presented with a series of carefully constructed poems, each exploring some aspect of the poet's unease. Place and personal history are used to throw into relief aspects of her relationship with England and with Pakistan and India. Rather than being cast into flawless ingots of claim and counter claim, her poems are presented unassumingly, questioning rather than stating. Titles like 'And If' and 'All There Is' have a disarming sense of artlessness. And many of the poems too, although sweetly constructed have a simple structure. Here's 'Rainy Season':

I scale the wall
walk the tightrope high above
the house where I was born.
The neighbourhood dips beneath me
and the wind blows.

Daytime the sky is white and cool
as a bowl of firni.
Night time it flows like a woman's hair.
I conjure up the rainy season, command each drop
set this house like an ark on the ocean.

Like many of Alvi's poems, it works because of what is left out and it is easy to imagine that it was in an earlier draft a longer and more complicated piece. If I had a criticism of this poem and of a very few other poems then it would be to suggest that they lack a certain drive, a certain tension. We are, perhaps, in danger of saying, *so what?* But if we don't take time to answer that question ourselves then it is the reader who is not doing the poem justice. And it would be unkind, because there are many poems in this collection that are wonderfully potent. 'Lahore Canal', for instance, is a little pressure cooker of a poem with a revealing and entertaining jab at the difficulty of reading the English novel without being entirely aware of all it's cultural (and meteorological!) assumptions. And of course it says a lot more. Lets just say it's about heat and leave it at that.

Alvi is very good on cities. The first section has a number of poems that explore her memories of cities and her feelings on returning. Closed rooms, courtyards, streets, bazaars are background to the comparisons she makes between South Asia and England. The marvellous poem 'Delhi Christmas', perhaps because it is less directly personal, gives us a wonderfully cool and objective picture of the curious juxtaposition of India with the stifling calm of an English Christmas. The final line, "English couples talk of cats in Abingdon", is so perfect it is almost cruel! The poem 'Story of a City' is the culmination of these city poems. In twenty seven lines she takes the idea of a city and unravels it ("it seemed to be / just stuffed and stuffed inside itself") to reveal it as "the named / and nameless threats, the interlocking worlds".

Rather than a single vision, Alvi makes use of glimpse after glimpse to infuse her poems with a marvellous luminosity. 'The Airborne House', concludes with: "Tiger, the labrador bought from Harrods / / trouble with his back legs, / stumbles through the airborne cool / / and sinks down on the marble floor". That light touch, more than perhaps the surrealism of other poems, gives this collection its strength.

W. N. Herbert's

Cabaret McGonagall is an all singing, all dancing book, as the title might suggest. Not that McGonagall is Herbert's muse – and how well he knows we know that – but only one of many characters enlisted by Herbert in fighting his good fight. Satire is the current of air that runs through the collection, and satire was never much good at being private or contemplative. Everyone and everything is up for a good going over. Even, of course, the poet himself, most entertainingly in the short final poem 'Answermachine'.

Cabaret McGonagall is constructed in five sections, covering the compass points in their titles and with an extra one for the north. Each has a couple of introductory quotes (for instance the chirpy: "Mrs Carritt, my tea tastes like tepid piss" – W. H. Auden) and each is given a sense of being constructed as part of an argument. This will not suit casual readers, those who start at the end of books or in the middle. But then, what Herbert presents us with is his various vision of a various world where each part needs the other to make the whole. Despite an occasional postured carelessness he is taking the whole thing seriously.

This is his strength, a belief that poem after poem delivered with such confidence will deliver to the reader a smack in the mouth from the ludicrous world. It makes for uneasy reading, especially for an Englander. Reference is hitched to reference – contemporary, pre-history, fact, fiction – until I hardly knew what was going on. He is a driven poet, driven to leave nothing out in his twitching pursuit of summing the whole thing up. I came away from the first reading feeling overwhelmed, guilty that I had surely missed or misunderstood so much but irritated that Herbert had kept up such a furious pace. The title poem, 'Cabaret McGona-gall', is leaning over the front of the stage screaming at the audience. Here's the first stanza:

> Come aa ye dottilt, brain-deid lunks,
> ye hibernatin cyber-punks,
> gadget-gadjies, comics-geeks,
> guys wi perfick rat's physiques,
> fowk wi fuck-aa social skills,
> fowk that winnae tak thir pills:
> *gin ye cannae even pley fuitball*
> *treh thi Cabaret McGonagall*

Sure, I'm uneasy because I fit the bill on two or three counts, but I'm also uneasy because I don't know how all this is going to turn out. Which, I hope, is just the reaction Herbert wanted. For all the right reasons this stuff is not destined for GCSE exam papers. If it is cabaret then they've closed the bar during the first set and there are some big blokes on the door discouraging departure. And there's serious feedback from the p.a.

With the enormous range of Herbert's material there are some extraordinarily funny poems. 'Why the Elgin Marbles Must Be Returned to Elgin' is marvellous ("Because local building contractors would use / JCBs to play giant games in Cooper

Park / and attract more tourists to Morayshire: / 'Monster Marble Showdown Time!'"). The prose section in the sequence 'Road Movie' is a rumination on a marriage between Hollywood and the Scottish Borders ("The angel dreams of how Hollywood could have loved the legendary showdown between the Douglases and the Percies in *Gunfight at Otterburn Paddock*").

Almost every poem in the collection seems to have been infused with a real inventiveness. There are *no* set pieces, *no* poems that will surely win poetry competitions because they cover all the bases and offend no one. The poetry is immediate, happily rough around the edges, contemporary, public and proud of it. What I believe I learnt after living with these poems for a while is that they are actually built for performance. I have seen the man on stage with some of these poems and he knows exactly what he is doing. And the twists and turns of the poems really need his voice and its direction to reveal themselves to an audience or reader. Buy the book. Go to the reading.

The Habitations of Desire?

by Helen Kidd

Poetry in the British Isles: Non-Metropolitan Perspectives

eds. Hans-Werner Ludwig and Lothar Fietz,
University of Wales Press, £14.95,
ISBN 0 7083 1266 7

DIVIDED INTO THREE sections, this collection of essays provides historical and cultural discussion, against which investigations of the relationship of poetry to particular places, communities, gender, identity and linguistic variety might develop. The unstated position is a Liberal Humanist one which incorporates a plurality of voices, but tends to exclude radical theorising about the psychodynamics of community and artistic/linguistic utterance. I fell on this volume with enthusiasm, found useful material, but also felt frustrated by its limitations.

No doubt the book will prove invaluable as a starting point for enthusiasts of poetry of place, and as a stepping stone for students of particular regional literatures, and is very informative. The first section traces established canonical links to the hegemonic view of the periphery, as it developed in England from the Renaissance period to 1800. It outlines dominant discourses on national and cultural identity, and literature's complex relationship to this. There is a cohesion here as Fietz and Ludwig are both concerned with matters of cultural history.

The second section, on specific regions and literatures, beginning with a rather superficial overview of 'Place in Modern English Poetry' by Jeremy Hooker, is rather more bony. The essayists are a mixture of poets, editors and academics, and there is an over-emphasis on themes and imagery at the expense of language and form. Poetry from Wales in English and Welsh, Hiberno-English and Irish writing, and in Scots and Scots Gaelic are also given consideration. A number of important poets are examined, and, inevitably, a number are omitted. I find myself wondering at the lack of Black and Asian writers, whose double focus adds both to linguistic variety of other englishes, and to new perspectives on community and national identities. I also regret the absence of challenging and innovative women writers such as Wendy Mulford and Denise Riley. These might have been usefully included in Hooker's essay where he gives consideration to Basil Bunting. It has to be said that the complexities of Bunting's blurred boundaries between subject and community, the public and the private, revealed in his layers of history and mythos in the North East, is really only glossed here. Hooker begins promisingly with Green issues raised by Kim Taplin's work, but drifts into a synopsis of different thematic concerns, as does an essay on Welsh poets by Alban Davies. Wynn Thomas, however, does allow for a discussion of form and language in work by poets such as Robert Minhinnick, Mike Jenkins, and Peter Finch, whose "quintessential Welsh wordscapes [render the] language issue . . . a primary fact of life that makes the English language visible and tangible in a way it rarely can be in 'purely' English society". I wanted more of this kind of observation, which he does well, both here and throughout the collection.

The final section comprises five studies of individual poets' works, two white English males, one Welsh speaking male, one male Scot, and Gillian Clarke. One night lament the absence of an Irish poet here, but for Sabina Sharkey's excellent essay on Irish language poetry, which also compensates for the lack of in-depth attention to women poets elsewhere. Alban gestures towards the new women poets writing in Welsh, and Derick S. Thomson nods in the direction of Gaelic poets Meg Bateman, Mary and Catriona Montgomery (why the anglicised spelling?) with the throwaway line "Feminism and greenness break through the heather".

So many issues inform the subject of place that a coherent theory is pressingly necessary. The relationship of language to community, gender and class is everywhere implicit, but nowhere discussed with any methodological rigour, with the exceptions of Sharkey's 'And not just for Pharoah's daughter: Irish language poetry today' and Hargreaves' 'Tony Harrison and the poetry of Leeds'. Both of these investigate the complexities of the relationships between poetry, language and place, both metropolitan and regional. They problematise their subjects, skilfully recognising the matrix of issues and contexts which reveal themselves at the level of register, linguistic choices and form. They demonstrate a concern with the social construction of the human subject within a linguistic landscape rooted in place. This involves, necessarily, absence and loss, before creative revisioning can take place.

Rainer Lengeler's essay on Charles Tomlinson gestures in this direction despite itself. Again thematic concerns are explored, but Tomlinson's repeated use of space and plenitude – which she notes – could have become an exposition of his very postmodernist re-evaluation of perception and cognition. The poet's intention is less interesting than the poetry itself, with its refreshing self-referentiality; those recurrent images of black and white etchings, lines, parallax, and space, indicate a poetic sensibility tuned to the fluid gestures of language, which Lengeler so skilfully itemises in her close reading of his work, but traps in a transcendentalism which fails to do justice to his sense of surfaces and the senses; decentring controlling specularity and reformulating space as potential.

Literatures which rest as much on the oral as the visual properties of their material need some acknowledgement. David Annwn's rather hagiographical study of MacKay Brown and Derick S. Thomson's 'Poetry in Scottish Gaelic, 1945–1992'

might have benefited from more discussion of the influence of oral culture on Scottish Literature. Thomson acknowledges its part as cultural background, but fails to indicate the bowdlerisation and fixity which the written word has imposed on ballad and lyric traditions, and the appropriation of women's poetic forms that this has involved.

Thomson's essay left me feeling satisfied in particulars but frustrated by the lack of an argument, whereas Kimpel on contemporary Scottish poetry is all of a piece, highly informative and lucid, and benefits greatly by using post-colonial theorists Ashcroft, Griffiths and Tiffin as a springboard into her discussion. Her argument that the places between cultures should be defined precisely leaves me wanting more, for such places might include poets missing from her essay; Black and/or women writers for example. Where do Jackie Kay, Maud Sulter or Kathleen Jamie figure in her argument or, on the male side, W. N. Herbert and his plurality of voices and tongues? Kimpel covers poets already much written about. No crime, but rather narrow. This is also the case for Garrat's study of Irish poetry in English (but less true for the Welsh language writers). But, once again, where are the women, McGuckian and Boland to name but two? Where also are those with an eye and ear to the specificities of dialect (Paulin and Carson spring to mind)?

The collection introduces a wide range of poets, from Ned Thomas' piece on Waldo Williams for example, to Annwn's list of island writers from other parts of the world. Harvie's preface provides an interesting introduction (despite his misleading use of the term "waulking"), but alas, the material did not live up to my expectations. I lament the persistent use of the generic "man" throughout the volume, and am surprised at editors accepting the term, although it is in keeping with the unexamined masculinist bias; despite K. E. Smith's sympathetic feminist reading of Gillian Clarke, which partly redresses the balance. The discussion is still young, and what is needed is an examination of the psychodynamics of desire in relation to place (including nostalgia *and* alienation) and how poetic language becomes an evocation, substitution, celebration of, and struggle with that internal, as well as geographical and sociological, topos. Poetry of place is poetry of the site of desire, and I desire more on desire.

Helen Kidd is the author of *Calemadonnas, Women and Scotland* (Gairfish, 1994), essays on Scottish women writers.

Déjà Vu

by Toby Litt

JULIA COPUS
The Shuttered Eye
Bloodaxe, £6.95,
ISBN 852243384

ALTHOUGH JULIA COPUS' *The Shuttered Eye* is a first collection, it already feels very familiar – and not in a wholly positive way. The reason for this familiarity is that almost all the poems fall into one or other sub-genre. There are the Poems That Rewrite Something Else: Fairytales ('Little Red-Cap', 'Hansel's Dream'); The Book of Genesis ('The Making of Eve'); Homer ('Passing By the Sirens'); A Character from a Novel ('Miss Havisham's Letter'); A Painting ('Massacio's Expulsion from Paradise', 'The Scream'). There are the Poems About Traumatic Experiences: Anorexia ('The Smallest Room'), Mastectomy ('Breast'), Rape ('The Door'), Caesarean Birth ('Cut'). There is the Poem About Harvesting Something: ('Nutting'). And – yes, you guessed – there is the Poem i.m. Sylvia Plath ('Courage'). Nothing about this is necessarily wrong. It is perfectly acceptable for a first collection to demonstrate a familiarity with and an indebtedness to what has gone before. But by writing in so many familiar sub-genres, Copus cannot help raising the question of how she compares to their previous exponents – and to their originators. "Here is a new poet", we say to ourselves, "What do they have to say – in this form, about this subject – that is new?"

The poem deriving from Munch's 'The Scream' is as good an example as any. The Screamer itself is now available from art shops as a sort of angsty blow-up doll. The painting itself has been stolen and recovered, to much media coverage. A work of art could hardly be more ubiquitous. So, how does Copus see it?

> The way is straight, say the flat-folk going about
> their business in their long greatcoats. The air hardly
> acknowledges them, they are so thin, and the road
>
> streams under their booted feet – a rush of tarmac,
> glistening, spectacular . . .

The poem is describing, interpreting and moralising the painting, all at the same time. The flat-folk are personified by their lack of personality, their insensibility: "... they do not see / the way the lights catch in it ...", "They do not look back / to where they've come from ...". Next, the speaker of the poem becomes or reveals themself as the subject of the painting:

> They do not see me, appearing from nowhere,
> as prophets do; little more than a ghost, a noiseless
>
> shadow with my long fingers, my yellow skull-face,
> the near-perfect O of my mouth.

There is a possibility of something original – and audacious – in the mention of prophets, but the thought is not followed up. The remainder of these lines are full of perfectly unobjectionable factual information – "long fingers", "the near-perfect O of my mouth" – and perfectly predictable associations – "ghost", "shadow", "skull". (Would you bother to read art criticism that merely said, "The face of the figure in Munch"s 'The Scream' reminds me of a skull"?) The poem concludes:

> Slowly now
> I form a tunnel with my hands to take my voice
>
> far far out . . . I scream; the flat-folk do not
> miss a step. Behind them the red sky seethes.

I'm sorry, but this is insufficient. In a book which takes sight as one of its main themes (the title poem is about gradual loss of eyesight), one has reason to expect a more interesting and distinctive vision.

Yet there are moments of promise, here and there. There is a formal bravado in 'The Back Seat of My Mother's Car' and 'Bomb' – poems which fold in the middle, the second half being an exact reversal of the lines of the first. 'The Last Days of Proverbia' is both witty and menacing:

> 6 am: the birds are out in force.
> Worms are caught. High up on the hill
> an ill wind is stirring; the tide
> is rising fast. Bridges are built
> and then crossed, with alarming speed.

And the final four poems of the book seem to have relaxed into a more distinctive point of view. If these are the most recently composed, Julia Copus' next collection should be something to look forward to.

THE SONNET HISTORY

JOHN WHITWORTH
CONCRETE AND CLAY

If Edwin Morgan were to wear this sonnet
He wouldn't wear it like a bowler hat
But with a rakish twist, the auld Scots bonnet
Like this . . .

or **THIS** . . .

or t h i s . . . or t

h

i

s

or . . .

. . . SPLATT!

AND*IAN*HAMILTON*FINLAY
WOULD*EMPLOY*INSTEAD
TEAK*BRASS*INLAY
AND*FLOWER*BED

but i would definitely say
the BIG DADDY of popular strummings
on the lyre of poetry is from the u s of a
(wait for it babe) ee cummings

of course there's archy & mehitabel
but wotthehell wotthehell

JOHN BURNSIDE
TALK OF THE DEVIL

That game we would play
with mirrors,

lighting a candle
and holding it up to the glass

to catch the fiend:
it must have begun as a way

of finding the others,
the husband concealed in the future, the ghostly

trawlermen,
too long away at sea.

In every parish women sprinkled fires
with salt, or tossed a bobbin to the night

and waited for the shapes
that love assumes,

but all we ever wanted was a moment's
danger, just a shiver at the edge

of vision, then a sense
of bristle or smiling bone, or a quiet

shifting away in the darkness
beyond the flame,

a spirit we might have followed
if we chose,

wandering out of the house
to God knows where.

KEITH JEBB
AUDIO ANIMATRONICS

the 'Enchanted Tiki Room'
talking birds and flowers,
kinky jungle thick and matted
into tortuous anti-braids

A zero had just dropped
off the end of her compassion
"you won't dream of spiders
any more" safety
over slippery enamel

At weekends boatloads of anoraks
hear the words
for staccato rain
on the brollies

anonymized with undiluted pleasure
in black and yellow cubicles
sprouted in every town and village

The annulospiral sensory endings
of normal muscle spindles
                    flower-spray
          a succession of rings

Anna Hummingbirds with
rose-red gorgets
in suitable light
Belinda is let loose
in the vertebrate house

plug-minded bibbity-boo
glides through the waters
of six continents

DREW MILNE
NIGHT NIGHT

A goose bump shrinks
from high, bare places
to a stung, prone oh so

supine hem, its lounge
short of fiery loam but
tuned to fine leaves of

ouch. We're rapt, even
as a sang rind and bark
enskies the miraculous.

So off with flits to an
inkling sulk, to glitter
for a pouring crag of

scoffed milk. Unsew
such spurious sorts to
ring in sweet chunder

or snores. If and only
if turns a lip canopy on
its fetchingly high side.

Now rends out to deck
its joy boy, he of craven
dances, skirts and crust

cuts of mister bombast
scooping up scars in the
scouring. Be our sleep

collar, be our iron hum
to none, done for by the
moon in gorgeous bone.

No, that brags it most
which throws to wake
off this filching. You

are some clear day, as
the yoke singes into its
neck. Spoons chrome

to chamber lines, white
trash all but blown into
love oer the core sloth.

Well, that makes some
crime of it, or simpers
into a windy but vogue

harangue, so sparkling
to the lees. Go swift to
dull, buds that oh stills

to trimmers or breaking
bounds, that optimum
slurp clasped in a pyre.

GRETA STODDART

DUNGENESS

HOME OF THE LATE DEREK JARMAN

A man in a black shirt is kneeling in a garden.
He is holding a handful of seed. He looks up.
The sun is humming like a low engine
and all around acres and acres of earth
erupt in sudden tufts of grass
as dry and sparse as sick mens' hair,
And the lighthouse is haunted with the cries of men
who mistook its wink for a welcome.

Sand sieves through the scalp of a doll
whose despised body lies scattered, in bits.
She doesn't know how to die but she's trying.
And the little houses sit like accidents,
their windows broken, their doors open,
guarded by gnomes with hurtful smiles.

Orange iron tracks stop one foot short
of the water's edge. The final carriage
has long since tipped itself down
onto the ocean floor where it's turning
now into a quiet and complicated home
for the fish who pass unflinchingly by.

On the shore the corpse of a baby shark
lies on its back, its cold eye
still seeing, and its penis, open, curls
in surprise on its tender white belly.
In the hollows of dunes happy sofas
sit and wait like patient guests.

And in that garden three black shirts
hang on a line. The man is planting now.
There's an element of shame in the way he bows
his head as he buries the excited buds
deep and deeper under the earth.
He wonders if he'll touch the sleeve, or the collar
or even the lips of his safely dead lover.
And the lighthouse is haunted with the cries of men
who mistook its wink for a welcome.

KEVIN CROSSLEY-HOLLAND
WHITE NOISE

Night swallows fumes from the mouth of the stack,
    and dusty knots
of creeper that half-covers the brick are sealed
    with ice.
Lowering your voice, you talk about fireflies, all
    kinds of owls,
dim creatures on the slimy bed that never swim,
    they reach and slide.
The standard first and then seven tulips long-necked
    in the window:
you turn off all the lights to hear the sound of
    falling snow.
All we hear at first are the animal sounds of
    ourselves
– our hearts' iambs, and blood whistling round our
    heads, our coarse breathing.
And snow that past midnight we scarcely see falling
except on an uptide, dancing on our window ledge,
    continues to fall.

Outside and shapeless, we shuffle like ancients
    block to block ...
This wind's from the east: cottonwoods blossom,
    chastened cars
take the veil, and each cable fitting wears a busby
    and plume.
Motors and treads, party laughter on the doorstep,
    the tolling bell:
they're dampered like dreams, they sound like
    memories of themselves.
A muffler's laid over the whole huge engine of
    the city.
Immoderacy! I slip and drift, and believe we have
    no destination
and will never reach one, and that's only the
    beginning.
There is something white stars say to you
and you throw off all the night to hear the sound
    of falling snow.

As we walk the watches, still the underhum withdraws,
exhausts and conditioners, fans and vents withdraw
until in the hour before dawn there is this:
this almost nothingness;
you, floating;
the sound of silence deepening, which is white noise.

BACK NUMBERS

Please photocopy this page, ticking the issues you require. UK prices are as follows: Vol 80 – £3.00 plus 50p p&p; Vol 81 – £3.95 plus 50p p&p; Vols 82 and 83 – £4.50 plus 50p p&p, Vols 84 and 85 – £4.95 plus 50p p&p. Postage on 2 copies – 80p; 3 copies – £1.40; 4 or 5 copies – £2.65. For overseas add an extra £1.00 to the above.

❏ **SERMONS IN STONES**
(Vol 86 No 2, 1996)
Gwyneth Lewis on Metaphor; Paul Bailey on T. S. Eliot and anti-Semitism; Fiachra Gibbons on Seamus Heaney; Philip Gross on J. H. Prynne; poems by Paul Muldoon, Donald Davie, Michael Donaghy, Helen Dunmore, Ruth Sharman.

❏ **HOW THE CENTURY LOST ITS POETRY**
(Vol 86 No 1, 1996)
Peter Forbes on Modernism; Edna Longley on 20th Century anthologies; Ian Sansom on Auden; poems by David Gascoyne, Moniza Alvi, Roger McGough, Tessa Rose Chester.

❏ **THE POETRY MAP**
(Vol 85 No 4, 1995/96)
Gwyneth Lewis on bilingualism; Mandelstam Street – from the KGB Archives; Paul Bailey on Auden; poems by Fleur Adcock, Helen Dunmore, Zsuzsa Rakovszky.

❏ **POETRY FOR CHRISTMAS**
(Vol 85 No 3, 1995)
41 Best Buys; Peter Forbes: Why the New Popular Poetry Makes More Sense; poems by Tony Harrison, Fleur Adcock, John Fuller, U. A. Fanthorpe, Kit Wright.

❏ **THE COUNTRY AT YOUR SHOULDER**
(Vol 85 No 2, 1995)
International issue. Poems by Charles Simic, Czeslaw Milosz, Moniza Alvi, Durs Grünbein, Miroslav Holub, John Berger. Nick Hornby on Glyn Maxwell.

❏ **STILL LIFE AT THE POETRY CAFE**
(Vol 85 No 1, 1995)
Penguin Modern Poets launch: Duffy, Maxwell, Wright, Feaver etc; Poetry & Science; Welsh poetry; poems by Lavinia Greenlaw, John Burnside, Keki N. Daruwalla.

❏ **CLASSIC/NATIONAL POETRY DAY**
(Vol 84 No 3, 1994)
Poems by Hardy, Larkin, Stevie Smith, Eliot, Graves; Versions of Ovid: Hughes, Heaney, Lasdun.

❏ **LIFEWORKS**
(Vol 84 No 2, 1994)
John Mortimer on Betjeman; Adrienne Rich interviewed; Lavinia Greenlaw on Elizabeth Bishop.

❏ **NEW GENERATION POETS**
(Vol 84 No 1, 1994)
Bumper 128 page issue: Armitage, Burnside, Donaghy, Duffy, Duhig, Garrett, Greenlaw, Herbert, Hofmann, Jamie, Maxwell, McKendrick, Paterson, Stainer etc.

❏ **POETS ON POETS**
(Vol 83 No 4, 1993/94)
Seamus Heaney on Frost, Peter Porter on Auden, Stephen Romer on Eliot; poems by Wendy Cope, Kathleen Jamie.

❏ **THIRTEEN WAYS OF LOOKING AT TSVETAEVA**
(Vol 83 No 3, 1993)
Tsvetaeva versions by Carol Ann Duffy, Carol Rumens, Jo Shapcott, Carole Satyamurti et al; Stephen Spender on Wilfred Owen; poems by John Ashbery, Jean Joubert, Susan Wicks, Fred D'Aguiar, Jane Duran.

❏ **THE DANCER AND THE DANCE**
(Vol 83 No 2, 1993)
Bloodaxe's The New Poetry and new work by Debjani Chatterjee, Gerard Woodward, Lavinia Greenlaw, Paul Durcan; David Kennedy: Poetry & Science; Michael Hulse on political poetry.

❏ **IN SEARCH OF KAVITA**
(Vol 83 No 1, 1993)
Peter Forbes in India; Stephen Spender on Dom Moraes; John Bayley on Tagore; Carol Rumens on Kamala Das; Sudeep Sen on new Indian poets; poems by Daruwalla, Mahapatra.

❏ **SONGLINES/NOT JUST KIDS' STUFF**
(Vol 82 No 4, 1992/93)
Glyn Maxwell, William Scammell, Leon Rosselson, Jeremy Reed on poetry & song; Helen Dunmore, Philip Gross on children's poetry.

❏ **NEW POETS '92**
(Vol 82 No 3, 1992)
Poems by Susan Wicks, W. N. Herbert, Edward Deville, Aileen La Tourette, Marita Maddah, Ian Gregson, Sophie Hannah; Peter Levi on Ted Hughes.

Please send me the issues I've ticked.

I enclose a cheque for £

Name: _____

Address: _____

_____

_____

Please return photocopy and remittance to:
Poetry Review, 22 Betterton Street, London WC2H 9BU.

Margin allies

by Elaine Feinstein

ROY FISHER
The Dow Low Drop:
New and Selected Poems
Bloodaxe, £8.95,
ISBN 1 85224 340 6

CHRISTOPHER MIDDLETON
Intimate Chronicles
Carcanet, £8.95,
ISBN 1 85754 227 4

OF THE TWO POETS under review Roy Fisher is the more directly accessible. There's no mistaking the zinc light on his urban landscapes, nothing literary in a shift coming off work from the Lucas lamp factory on a Summer night or a man in a blue suit facing into a corner, straddling to keep his shoes dry. His is the landscape of the industrial Midlands, particularly Birmingham, where the sunlight has the gleam of lead soldiers, and his people move about in it with the ambiguous cheerfulness of figures in an L. S. Lowry painting. Middleton is an altogether more difficult poet. His chronicles are not autobiography in the ordinary sense, but the record of a subtle mind, mulling over the archaeology of its own growth. His intimate discoveries have to be dug out, layer below layer of artefact and myth, language and history.

At first sight then, there is little these poets have in common. Yet their techniques for controlling cadence, their ear for syllables set against one another were invented at a time when such skills were unfamiliar enough for their work to be relegated to the margins. Both poets were open to Charles Olson, Black Mountain, the early Objectivists and New York Surrealism, a brew enriched in Fisher's case by his love of jazz, and in Middleton's by his knowledge of French and German poetry.

The personality that emerges from Fisher's poetry, for all these influences, is altogether English: ironic, humorous, self deprecating and unpretentiously local. He wears the influence of William Carlos Williams lightly. When he opens Williams' *Pictures from Breughel* an entirely physical odour of currants trapped between the pages rises from the book and triggers a poem; rather as a poem rose from Williams' note of apology to his wife after eating cold plums from the fridge.

Fisher's honesty is playful, however much his imagery arises so directly from experience. In an early poem, 'After Working', for instance, he writes about the pleasures of squatting on a patch of city grass when tired and finding,

> The thoughts I'm used to meeting
> at head height when I walk or drive
> get lost here in the petrol haze
> that calms the elm tops
> over the sun set shadows I sit among.

His later poems are spikier, more deliberately awkward, as if he came to dislike a music that could cover and make comfortable what ought to pain. Through obduracy, discomfort and trouble, as he writes in 'Wonders of Obligation' he has come over a lifetime to recognise that "my life keeps / leaking out of my poetry to me / in all directions". Even in his earliest work the melody is never there only to please the senses. When he writes unsentimentally of a dying relative the music works as a way of conveying to his reader the daze of hospital watchers:

> As he came near death, things grew shallower for us.
> We'd lost sleep, and now sat muffled in the scent of
> tulips, the medical odours and the street sounds,
> going past, going away.

A poem he used to enjoy performing on the Seventies reading circuit was a wry acknowledgement of the difficulty he found in keeping his books in print, and takes the form of a letter, from the writer of a thesis on his works, who is unable to obtain texts:

> It is too late for me to change
> my subject to the work
> of a more popular writer, so please Mr Fisher
> you must help me . . .

Now that a substantial selection of his work is safely back in print, his historical position seems assured; more importantly, he is still writing.

Christopher Middleton

The excellence of Christopher Middleton's translations from German are widely known, and have perhaps distracted attention away from a poet who had his first book out more than fifty years ago when he was 19, and has never stopped producing work of originality. These 'Intimate Chronicles' reveal a more cosmopolitan sensibility than Fisher. Although he has lived and worked in the United States for many years, Middleton's surrealism is altogether European; and his take is global, often disturbingly so. A dromedary chomps outside a saloon in a country of banana plants, for instance. There are signs of his affection for Edward Lear, a passionate interest in nineteenth century explorers and archaeologists, and an omnipresent awareness of Classical Greek myth. He brings together place and person with as free a disregard for historical time as any writer of science fiction.

An example of this, and one of the most affecting poems in this collection is 'The Old Tour Guide – His Interpreter'. A visitor is being taken round a Greek house in present day Turkey, down a staircase, into a crypt where there is a luminously beautiful painting of Christ, and further downwards, while the tour guide comments and ruminates. There is a valley with a clear stream and a willow bush, and then suddenly it becomes possible that the tour guide is Odysseus himself, never returned to Ithaca; an Odysseus who had in an unimaginable longevity stretching from Homer to the time of Mohammed, converted to Islam.

> Wait, what wild talk is this
> of war striking a far country … stored at home his
> great bow?
> Seven times I heard the suffix
> which in his language indicates hearsay.

The poem concludes with an Islamic blessing, as if the whole descent through the house has been a quest for that revelation. The search for the numinous is a constant theme in all Middleton's poems, and its frustration is often expressed in exasperation, as much with himself as the world around him:

> All your theologies, all, are fragments
> From Aphrodite's shattered mirror

– he reflects in 'Catacombs'. That is why he prefers to look for the numinous in things themselves: implements, coins, even people going about their specialised tasks. Hence his delight in the papermaker in Berlin Pankow who breaks down the fibres of old camisoles and shifts to reproduce the paper of ancient etchings; or his enjoyment at puzzling over an old photograph of Chekhov and his brother. Yet the things he so delights to name are often strewn over the ground of his poems rather as they might be found in an archaeologists' dig; that

is to say without the articulations of a syntax which could relate one layer of discovery to the next. They demand a love of exploration equal to that of the poet, which has to be pursued with same passion in the hope of a spiritual revelation. A similar aspiration may lie hidden behind Middleton's love for paradox and the play of words – "I blow the candle out. / Here I goat (sic) to sleep".

The second section of this book, which deals with artistic epiphanies is filled with less arcane pleasures: the skaters in the Luxembourg gardens,

> Ankles turning as they try to move,
> Two of the women wear such ponderous hats.
> Shaping her mouth, narrowing her eyes
> Another shoots an ecstatic look, at what?

And there are even some poems which are altogether of this world: one called 'Some Dogs' for instance, which after evoking blue skies, poplars and olive trees, and a Frenchman in his café muttering "fils de pute" ends with the description of a single dog:

> He looks around
> One thought obliterating in that instant
> Every single smell or sound in his neighbourhood:
> My dish was full, now I have licked it clean.

These simplicities are not characteristic. At his best, Middleton's lines have a rhetoric as compelling in its way as Ashbery's. In 'Thirst Confessed' for instance, "What is this mirage if not intent / To lift the shimmer up, give tongue to it / In a tongue its time has thickened".

What was thought of as "free verse" when these two poets began to write was by and large Eliotic; that is to say, a music that depended on rhythmical expectations set up and then by turns frustrated and gratified. Both Fisher and Middleton found the shape of their poems instead in the rhythms of their own voice. This was a prosody which always carried some philosophical dangers, and the notation itself was problematic. William Carlos Williams once growled that no-one who had not heard him read could be relied upon to hear the crucial equality of time-length in his three-step line correctly. As it happens, neither of these poets needs to be heard aloud to be relished. Fisher is closer to the down-to-earth daily vision in which so much of poetry written now works best. Both are part of an unashamedly experimental tradition still available and still very much alive.

Wetting Appetites

by Judith Palmer

KATE CLANCHY
Slattern

Chatto, £6.99,
ISBN 07011 6332 1

NICKY RICE
Coming up to Midnight

Enitharmon, £6.95,
ISBN 1 870612 48 5

ALICE OSWALD
The Thing in the Gap-Stone Stile

Oxford Poets, £6.99,
ISBN 019 282513 5

SEX AND THE SINGLE girl stride brazenly into the slim volume in Kate Clanchy's debut collection, *Slattern*.

Upfront, in public as the sassy sophisticate, she basks in her power to bewilder the simple, unquestioning men who "don't know they're born, or why / born is hard, but snatch life smack from the sky, / a cricket ball caught clean that fills the hand" ('Men'). Yet at home mellowly, wistfully, she yearns and daydreams of "lying in someone's arms who says / he loves my eyes in French" ('Slattern').

One of the nine poets selected for Carol Ann Duffy's excellent *Anvil New Poets 2* last year, Clanchy has now found her way onto the Forward shortlist with her deft and distinctive collection of supple fantasies and lovelorn memories.

Her arch poems find their erotic charge in the gentlest situations: slipping a hand into a lover's shoes to feel the outline of an instep; watching his arms sunk to the wrist in the laundry basket, sorting sheets; or glowing with the proud conviction that her chap would be able to seize control in any emergency: "could set a dragging, broken leg, / one handed with two sticks / and a handkerchief".

Slattern's clammy, moist interior is unusually pungent, and I can think of few poets with a more keenly-developed nose for an evocative and revealing scent. She sorts out the men "smelling of wash that someone else has done" from the lonely boys "at the biscuit-smelling sour milk stage". 'Poem for a man with no sense of smell' sounds all the notes in her olfactory repertoire, informing the sensorily deficient for example,

> that the thickest line in the kink of my hand
> smells like the feel of an old school desk,
> the deep carved names worn sleek with sweat

The other real jewel of this collection is the lusciously tactile and wittily inventive 'The Wedding Guest's Story' in which a jilted man thrown over for a lycra-clad rock-climber, stares fixated at the nape of his beloved's neck, mentally making his ascent up "the low, secret steps of her spine /... scrambled sweating, swearing, / over the slopes of her shoulder blades, / to slump on the summit, weak, sobbing with loss".

If you're not in the right mood then *Slattern* will breeze flimsily past, but if romantically inclined, these fleeting brushes will make the hairs on your forearms crackle.

Nicky Rice

has been high up the medal table of the National Poetry Competition three times since 1980, winning first prize in 1990 with the poem 'Room Service'. Despite these successes, the Irish-born, Brighton-based poet has waited to cram over twenty years of writing into a satisfyingly substantial first collection, *Coming up to Midnight*.

Each poem is distinct and fairly attention-grabbing, suggesting Rice is most often galvanised into action by the arrival of a competition entry-form. That and finally winning a little time for herself on holiday. Her travel agent couldn't be better informed about her vacations and excursions than readers following the trail of her overnight bag: the me at Pompeii poem, the me at the Pyramids poem, the Greek island, Devon, the Yorkshire moors ...

One can feel a tad voyeuristic flipping through the writer's home photo album, complete with inadequate self-catering arrangements, capricious plumbing, night-time tears and mosquito bites. Lord, it's all a little too closely-observed. Particularly memorable is her 'Lament for Wilderness', recalling a particularly unmemorable bank-holiday daytrip: capturing a lacklustre outing in thin rain to a featureless resort ending with "tea in a garden somewhere". "Where does the past go when we have finished with it?" she asks. Her recollection of the day may be faint and fading fast, but these wafery impressions actually last longer than some of the showier poems.

Eminently anthologisable, Rice's poems present vigorously depicted situations: Cinderella thirty years on, nursing her bunions at the chiropodist's for example or the "bedsocks and barley water" world of the geriatric ward. There's a grand character sketch, too, of three ailing aunts who "dined out on their 'ops' for years, / for ill-health was something to be cultivated, / providing it was neither wet nor smelly".

The downside of her sense of the dramatic is a slight tendency towards the over-momentous summing-up ("And he looked at me and knew what he had lost"), awkward extended metaphor or forced pun, such as the limp worms which die quietly "making no bones about it".

Rice's world is vividly observed. Trying too hard to describe exactly what she's seen, however, she often breaks the flow of the poem to include an accurate image at the expense of a sinuous curve: a flowering cherry "effervesces" aptly but sadly discordantly, mice wait jarringly "agog". Rice thinks not feels her way into words, her ear for language a whisker off-pitch, despite an arrestingly distinctive voice and fascinated eyes.

Alice Oswald

is another of the burgeoning young writers showcased in the *Anvil New Poets 2* anthology to surge onto the Forward Prize shortlist. You won't find a more astounding first collection than *The Thing in the Gap-Stone Stile*

Paying debts to Hopkins, Herbert and Hughes, Oswald's landscape is hewn from moonshine and mudflats, granite and greenwoods. Early exercises in imitation, however, soon evolve into a complex and confident style of her own.

Oswald recites her seductively musical songs, ballads and sonnets from memory. Lush dew-drenched lines drip from the pages: "A spider swings from bloom to bloom. / A fungus detonates and slowly / leaf contusions rot to rheum" ('Poem'). Glasshouses hang with cucumber and "the long green lungs of that still air", the wind whips through cabbage nets, while peat-stained figures rush from sudden showers into musty pippin-lined potting sheds. The lines thrum with teeming, mutating, quickening life.

Oswald trained as a professional gardener with the Royal Horticultural Society at Wisley, and delights in the playful cross-pollination and grafting of images into metaphysical-style conceits. Occasionally the bond fails to take. Most often,

however, the emerging hybrid is sleek and startling.

Fascinated by the area "between", Oswald reflects on the territory she shares with a neighbour, a hedge that is both clipped and left "hippy" ('Privet Property'), or the disparate lives joined by a common chimney, "Our sitting rooms connect like shears / into the screw-pin of our fires" ('My neighbour, Mrs Kersey'). She skates on surface tension, peers through holey stones, losing herself in abstraction, yet always managing to re-ground herself, before she floats off into the metaphysical ether.

"Who's to say / whether or not the laws of quantities / apply at sea where everything is moving?" she questions in 'The Wise Men of Gotham', the breathtaking long poem (9 pages) which forms the cornerstone of the collection. Based on the medieval legend about three men who set out to sea, casting nets to catch the moon, this virtuoso piece is a truly fine work, evoking a spirit-laden seascape as potent as *The Rime of the Ancient Mariner*'s.

The sea spins into scimitars beneath, while ghostly forms spring "beating the flocks of horrid barking waves / towards this boat". One boatman "came shouting by / as if the art of thinking were a pommel / to pound the world into conformity", another "felt the hoops / of ice-cold sea contracting on his thighs". I could quote and quote from this astounding rhythmic torrent of spiralling images. Awesome.

NEWS/COMMENT

HALF-HIDDEN AGENDA

In the wake of the controversy regarding anti-Semitism in some of Eliot's poems, sparked off by Anthony Julius's *T. S. Eliot, anti-Semitism and literary form*, the question of Pound's politics has surfaced again, prompted not by a detractor but by Pound's staunchest defender William Cookson, editor of *Agenda*.

Some issues of the current number of *Agenda* carry an astonishing Note by Cookson, as a postscript to a review of *Sons of Ezra: British Poets and Ezra Pound*, edited by Michael Alexander and James McGonigal. I say *some* copies, because the Note was withdrawn from subsequent copies after co-editor Peter Dale and long-time contributor W. S. Milne resigned over the Note. Dale's (and presumably Milne's) resignation stands despite the withdrawal, and since the copy sent to *Poetry Review* contained no erratum slip or disclaimer of any kind we feel that the contents ought to be made known. It is quite clear that these are Cookson's views and that they were only withdrawn under pressure.

The Note is not even mainly a defence of Pound (although it is that): the real shock is that it is a defence of Mussolini: "it is time that the good, the positive and constructive actions of Mussolini, like, for example, his overthrowing of the Mafia, were given due weight ... It is often forgotten how much the Italian leader achieved towards 'the resurrection of Italy' during more than a decade of rule before the tragic embroilment with Hitler led to his downfall". Cookson makes it clear that he prefers Mussolini to the Allied leaders: "neither side in the Second War was innocent of 'crimes against humanity'. Of all those involved, Mussolini and the Italians were the least guilty in this respect. The German gas chambers, Hiroshima, Nagasaki, Dresden, the saturation bombing of German and Japanese cities, and the Russian massacre of Polish officers at Katyn were all acts of unprecedented barbarity – Churchill, Roosevelt, Truman and Stalin were guilty of criminal actions as well as Hitler". Of Pound himself, Cookson concludes: "Leaving aside the question of whether his opinions were right or wrong, Pound's courage in taking the microphone for his beliefs deserves our respect".

FORWARD PRIZES

This year the Forward Prizes will be announced on Wednesday 9 October, the eve of National Poetry Day. *The Forward Book of Poetry* will be published on the same day. The shortlist is as follows:

BEST COLLECTION

Charles Boyle, *Paleface*, Faber
(reviewed Vol 86 No 2, p85)
U. A. Fanthorpe, *Safe as Houses*, Peterloo
(reviewed Vol 85 No3, p7)
John Fuller, *Stones and Fires*, Chatto
(reviewed Vol 86 No 1, p73)
Seamus Heaney, *The Spirit Level*, Faber
(reviewed Vol 86 No 2, p44)
W. N. Herbert, *Cabaret McGonagall*, Bloodaxe
(reviewed this issue, p76)

BEST FIRST COLLECTION

Kate Clanchy, S*lattern*, Chatto
(reviewed this issue, p90)
Julia Copus, *The Shuttered Eye*, Bloodaxe
(reviewed this issue, p80)
Alice Oswald, *The Thing in the Gap-stone Stile*, Oxford Poets
(reviewed this issue, p90)
Ian Pople, *The Glass Enclosure*, Arc Publications
(reviewed this issue, p74)

BEST SINGLE POEM

Patricia Beer, 'Art History', *London Review of Books*
David Constantine, 'Bombscare', *Poetry Review*
(Vol 86 No 1, p41)
Maura Dooley, 'The Message', *The North*
Kathleen Jamie, 'The Graduates', *TLS*
Les Murray, 'The Early Dark', *The Rialto*

Besides David Constantine's 'Bombscare', the anthology will include three other poems first published in *Poetry Review*:

Harry Clifton, 'Reductio'
(Vol 86 No 1, p83)
Steve Ellis, 'Gardeners' Question Time'
(Vol 85 No 4, p57)
Kit Wright, 'All Purpose Country & Western Self Pity Song'
(Vol 85 No 3, p63)

NET VERSE

Blimey. This Internet thing really works! I had an e-mail the other day from Peter Horn in South Africa, asking if I'd like to mention his electronic magazine *Isibongo*. He'd heard about Net Verse from someone in America, and when I found the page, at **http://www.uct.ac.za/ projects/poetry/isibongo/isibongo.htm** it had, amongst other contributors, the very English Douglas Clark. When you visit, make sure to investigate the links to other South African writers.

Fast becoming an essential stopping-off point is Mary Lowry's Sacramento-based and award-winning *Poetic Express* at **http:/www.ns.net:80/ ~Lomar/mary3.htm** which has a constantly changing and eclectic content. She's issuing awards of her own now, so if you have a poetry site you're proud of, tell her about it.

Closer to home, Maggie Hannan's *Grim* was where Radio 4's Kaleidoscope dipped its toe. They didn't say where it was, though (and didn't know when I asked them), so if you're still wondering, try **http://adam.ac.uk/~maggie/Grim/** If you like your poetry uncompromising, wander north of the border to Rebel Inc. an underground literature and poetry site with some pretty strong stuff at **http://www.electricfrog.co.uk/rebelinc/ prom/scottish/underground/literature/poetry. htm**

Many poetry pages have links to others, of course, and these vary greatly in quantity and quality. One of the best is that maintained by Richard Soos, at **http://www.geocities.com/Paris/1416/** but if doesn't point you to enough sites to keep you occupied, then the On-line Literary Resources page at **http:/www.english.upenn.edu/~jlynch/ Lit** certainly will.

As page-builders become more skilled, and the facilities become available, resources on the Web become ever more versatile (and occasionally silly, but that's not the point.) For example, you can even find an on-line rhyming dictionary now, at **http://www.cs.cmu.edu/~dougb/rhyme.html** Don't expect it to find you a rhyme for purple, though. I would mention the anagram generator, at **http://csugrad.cs.vt.edu/~eburke/anagrams. html** but that *would be* silly.

Send me suggestions, sensible or silly, to the usual address: **peter@hphoward.demon.co.uk**

PETER HOWARD

NATIONAL POETRY DAY
THURSDAY 10 OCTOBER

The third annual National Poetry Day will put poets and poetry in the spotlight once again – on BBC TV and radio, in schools and colleges, arts centres and libraries around the UK. The organisers expect that National Poetry Day will again provide the impetus for a wide variety of impromptu readings and poetic activity at many venues.

BBC TV and radio will be broadcasting a wide range of programmes in the run-up to National Poetry Day. Griff Rhys-Jones, comedian and presenter of BBC TV's 'The Bookworm' will launch a new poll, inviting viewers to vote for the Nation's Favourite Poem of the Century.

Schoolchildren around the country will be encouraged to express themselves in verse and to celebrate poetry and the environment, thanks to the support of WWF-UK. The National Theatre in London stages 'Our World, Ourselves' – a week of performances on themes including: Samuel Beckett (Cottesloe, 7 Oct); War Poetry and Poetry of Conscience (Lyttleton, 10 Oct); The Environment (Cottesloe, 11 Oct); *Emergency Kit* (Cottesloe, 11 Oct). Booking office: 0171 928 2252.

COMPETITION

REPORT ON NO. 2:
HOMAGE TO CLICHÉS

You were asked for elaborated illustrations of worn-out phrases in the manner of Dickens. This seemed like a good idea at the time but the results suggest that the technique required has fallen into disuse since Dickens. Paul Groves scores few points for subtly disguising his phrase (most went to the other extreme) but at least he got a poem out of it.

En fin de compte

How close to midnight is this platitude,
Or does it just denote a trailing dusk,
The sigh of evening at this latitude
When what was bright and sharp becomes subfusc?

Finally, when all is nearly said
And nearly done, it comes into its own,
A terminal agreement, not the dead
Ground that lurks beyond the twilight zone

But the point when all accounts are squared,
All subtotals fashioned to a sum,
With every outcome clear and unimpaired,
Either for praise or for opprobrium

PAUL GROVES

NO 3: TENSE FODDER

The titles of pamphlets favoured by Iain Sinclair (see p3) remind us of Ian McMillan's poem, 'Some Poetry Presses I Shall Certainly Set Up Next Week'. Titles for pamphlets or presses wanted, preferably with an avant garde flavour. A selection of books of the season to be won. Deadline November 15th.

LETTERS

OBJECT LESSONS

Dear Peter Forbes,

I'm sorry, but Sheenagh Pugh's review of Eavan Boland's *Collected Poems* (Vol 86 No 2, p46) was simply inadequate. I really thought the bad old days were over, but no – here we have poetry wrought by a woman out of women's experience being dismissed as domestic trivia. This is not on.

During her flyting with John Hartley Williams, Sheenagh Pugh asked which was the worse – intentionally or unintentionally imperceptive criticism. Which indeed, and which was responsible for her own high handedness about this important poet?

I too find Eavan Boland's work problematic, but I am drawn to it. Every time I'm drawn to it, I ask myself – is Boland a wonderful, searching, risky poet, or is she a chancer who bedazzles a gullible American academy with the buzzwords at her disposal? She has a rich resource – Woman, Poet, Myth, Ireland. Love it or hate it, her work is certainly not intellectually empty.

Boland's line-endings are odd at times. She can seem cloth-eared. Her grammar irritates. The verb-less sentence. The occasionally lumpen portentousness and self-consciousness. But for all that, the *Collected Poems* reveal Boland's achievement as fascinating and on-going.

She has claimed and turned into poetry the real lives of many ordinary women; she is exploring the past silence of those women; her mother, grandmother, Irish women, all traditionally-employed women. The situations she writes from are female, albeit middle class, even wealthy. As are the *things:* fabrics and flowers, milk-bottles, babies, hawthorn. But there is war, and violence – she knows that the family is the first casualty. She has kept faith, and created a space and a voice which shows other women that the stuff of our lives is also the stuff of art, and that women can be the creators of poems, not merely their subjects.

Recently I read 'Object lessons' with a group of fifth-year school students (a poem about the breaking of a coffee mug, how banal, how trivial), and even they could do better than tell me that Boland was "into Ireland" or "heavily into mythology". Do I need to remind Pugh, a Celt, that there are mythologies other than the Greek? Boland's work, for good or ill, is suffused with myth, with Irishness. Can an Irish poet as acutely self-aware as Boland write *A time of violence* or *Outside History* without a nod at her own times? Don't the titles alone suggest something more than trivia?

Which brings us to the extraordinary claim that Boland's work is "not relevant". May I ask the obvious? Relevant to whom? And what does it mean for a poem to be "relevant"? Boland's work is relevant, if that means recognisable, to me and my life. Of what relevance is "relevance?" Is it "relevant" say, to hole up in a castle and write about angels? Are the resultant poems "relevant?"

In a final confusion of life with art we are told, bad-temperedly, that modern women "don't have time" to scent anything with lemon balm. This is a daft complaint. Most modern women (and men) "don't have time" to write poetry either. Boland's work is hardly intended as a companion to Mrs Beeton's. She has kept faith with the distaff side, and been rewarded with an opening into myth, history and identity which this writer finds enviable.

If all else fails, think of this – Eavan Boland's last three collections were all Poetry Book Society Choices. Does that not make Sheenagh Pugh consider that somewhere under the suffocating layers, something is going on?

A Collected Poems gives opportunity for an intelligent and insightful review, such, may I say, as was afforded the collections by the four Irish men. I am not only disappointed, but alarmed.

Yours sincerely,
KATHLEEN JAMIE
Newburgh,
Fife

MAN OF SUBSTANCE

Dear Peter Forbes,

In your lead piece ('Sermons in Stones', Vol 86 No 2, p3) you define a division in the literary world between those for metaphor & simile & those against – a we *v.* them division that seems more political than literary, especially as when reading further one sees it derives from your dogmatic claim that "such figures of speech are poetry's principal *raison d'être*".

What about all the splendid poems in our language without metaphors & similes? And in the poems with metaphors & similes, what about the spaces between? Are they merely metaphors & similes in preparation?

A characteristic of much second rate and superficial art is the mistaking of ornaments & devices for substance.

Another question. Disapproving of Ruskin, you dismiss him as a "true Victorian". Later you are extravagant in your praise of Dickens. Was he not then a "true Victorian"?

FRANK DUX
Bath

ALIENATED STONES

Dear Peter Forbes,

I read 'Sermons in Stones' with interest. Thank you for defending metaphor (and poor, abused cliché) against the "literal-minded". The bone I have to pick with you (aha!) has nothing to do with your general argument but with your references to "alienation", which you seem to interpret as the divorce of man from the physical world. This was such a minor part of your argument that it should not have evoked a letter – except that your definition of the term is in wide circulation today. And it is not exactly correct.

We must recall that the Greek term corresponding to "alienation" means "excluded from community", which is the sense in which twentieth century sociologists like Keniston use the word. However, the word – as it was introduced into the modern European consciousness – had a theological root. It specifically referred to the alienation ("alienus") of Lucifer and later, through the agency of Adam and Eve, the generational alienation of man from God. Further on, the term was refined to signify the soul/body split or the split between the sinful body and an independent free spirit. Then – in Augustine and Meister Eckhart – alienation assumed a positive as well as a negative meaning. The negative one was similar to the body/soul (blame-it-on-Eve) equation, but the positive one promised salvation if man "alienated" himself from bodily (physical) things. Here, for the first time, we come across the man/physical world equation – but in a different context.

The term continued to assume differing meanings in the eighteenth and nineteenth centuries, all of them based on the notion of "absence". These include Marx's economic definition of alienation and Kierkegaard's existential "definition" to quote just two. Anyway, the point I have been trying to make is that the current reduction of the meaning of alienation to a man/physical world equation is unwarranted and incorrect. This needs to be noted, for a lot of criticism of "alienation" as a tool of analysis is based on this limited and ahistorical definition of the term.

Best wishes and regards,
Yours sincerely,
TABISH KHAIR
Copenhagen,
Denmark

SOME CONTRIBUTORS

John Burnside's latest collection is *Swimming with the Flood* (Cape, 1995).

Stephen Burt writes for *Thumbscrew* and the *TLS*.

Kevin Crossley-Holland's latest collection, *The Language of Yes*, was published by Enitharmon this year.

Jonathan Davidson is Director of the Birmingham Readers' and Writers' Festival; his first collection, *The Living Room*, was published by Littlewood-Arc.

K. M. Dersley's *Fugitive Days* is forthcoming from Redbeck Press.

Hans Magnus Enzensberger's *Selected Poems* (Bloodaxe) was reviewed in *PR* Vol 84 No 2.

Elaine Feinstein's *Selected Poems* are published by Carcanet.

Thom Gunn's *The Man With Night Sweats* (Faber) won the first Forward Prize in 1992.

David Harsent's *Selected Poems* are published by Oxford Poets; a new collection will be published next year.

David Hart won the National Poetry Competition in 1994.

Selima Hill's latest collection is *A Little Book of Meat* (Bloodaxe, 1993).

Chris Jones won a Gregory Award this year.

Keith Jebb's study of Housman is published by Seren.

James Knowlson is Samuel Beckett's authorised biographer.

Rutger Kopland's *A World Beyond Myself*, translated by James Brockway, was published by Enitharmon in 1993.

Toby Litt's first novel, *Adventures in Capitalism*, was published by Secker & Warburg this year.

Edna Longley's *The Living Stream: literature and revisionism in Ireland* was published by Bloodaxe in 1994.

Jamie McKendrick's latest collection is *The Kiosk at the Brink* (Oxford Poets, 1993).

Ian McMillan's latest collection is *Dad, The Donkey's on Fire* (Carcanet, 1995).

Drew Milne teaches at the University of Sussex.

Edwin Morgan's *Collected Poems* were published in paperback by Carcanet earlier this year.

Sharon Olds' latest collection, *The Wellspring* (Cape), was reviewed by Deryn Rees-Jones in *PR* Vol 86 No 1.

Judith Palmer is publicist for the South Bank Centre's Literature Department and a freelance journalist.

Ian Sansom writes for the *Guardian, London Review of Books* and *Thumbscrew*.

Goran Simic saw out the siege of Sarajevo; he wrote the libretto for Nigel Osborne's operetta, *Europe*, performed in Sarajevo in February 1995.

Piotr Sommer is an editor of the Polish magazine *Literatura na Swiece*.

Anne Stevenson's *Collected Poems* (Oxford Poets) will be reviewed in the next issue.

John Tranter is the co-editor (with Philip Mead) of *The Bloodaxe Book of Modern Australian Australian Poetry*.

John Whitworth's *Sonnet History of Contemporary Poetry*, with illustrations by Gerald Mangan, will be published by Peterloo in 1997.

John Hartley Williams's *Ignoble Sentiments*, prose memoirs and fiction, was published by Arc in 1995.